TRANSPORTATION
AND THE
EARLY NATION

TRANSPORTATION AND THE EARLY NATION

PAPERS PRESENTED AT AN INDIANA AMERICAN REVOLUTION BICENTENNIAL SYMPOSIUM

Allen County–Fort Wayne
Historical Society Museum
Fort Wayne, Indiana
April 24–26, 1981

Indianapolis
Indiana Historical Society
1982

CONTENTS

ACKNOWLEDGMENTS

The fourth Indiana American Revolution Bicentennial Symposium was held in Fort Wayne at the Allen County-Fort Wayne Historical Society Museum, April 24–26, 1981, sponsored by the Indiana American Revolution Bicentennial Commission, the Indiana Historical Society, the Allen County-Fort Wayne Historical Society, and the Department of History at Indiana University-Purdue University at Fort Wayne. Arrangements for the symposium were made by the Historical Programming Committee of the Bicentennial Commission, Gayle Thornbrough, Indiana Historical Society, chairman; Pamela J. Bennett, Indiana Historical Bureau; Donald F. Carmony, Indiana University; David Crosson, Allen County-Fort Wayne Historical Society; John F. Stover, Purdue University; Aurele Violette, Indiana University-Purdue University at Fort Wayne; and George M. Waller, Butler University. Irene D. Neu, Indiana University, was most helpful in planning the program.

The work of the local co-ordinators of the program under the direction of David Crosson is gratefully acknowledged. The cruise on Fort Wayne's historic three rivers and the illustrated lecture, "The Wabash and Erie Canal Today," by Thomas and Julia Meek of Fort Wayne added much to the occasion.

TRANSPORTATION
AND THE
EARLY NATION

The Transportation Revolution and American Law: Constitutionalism and Public Policy

Harry N. Scheiber

The Transportation Revolution—a series of technological innovations in communications, each innovation sparking a wave of new investment and a set of sweeping economic changes—transformed the American national economy in the first half of the nineteenth century. It is not surprising, therefore, that the issue of "internal improvements" (as contemporaries termed transportation projects) should have been exceeded by no other issue, not even the slavery question, in its persistence or prominence in political discourse from 1815 to 1850. At the national level, demands from many quarters for an active federal role in internal improvements raised important questions as to state-national relationships, the constitutional basis for federal action, and the expediency of federal aid. At the state level, too, the Transportation Revolution confronted lawmakers with important issues concerning the legitimate reach and uses of governmental power. In state constitutional conventions, the legislatures, and state courts, no less than in the national government's lawmaking agencies, the legal system came under strain as it responded to the demands and aspirations of what one Indiana state judge, in language typical of the day, termed "this age of improvement."[1]

For the people of the Old Northwest in particular, the constitutional and legal controversies inspired by the Transportation Revolution were the subject of intense concern. The economic prospects

Harry N. Scheiber is Professor of Law in the University of California, Berkeley. This paper was prepared for the symposium, but, because of illness, Professor Scheiber was unable to present it at Fort Wayne.

I

of the region beyond the Appalachians clearly depended both upon the improvement of communications through the mountain barrier and upon safe, low-cost navigation of the Great Lakes and the interior's river system. Hence, the issue of internal improvements— especially federal aid for western transportation projects—stood at center stage in regional politics in the early period of promotion, from 1815 to the mid-1820s, and thereafter in the great sectional drama that went on until 1861.[2] Westerners consistently pressed for Congress to make grants of cash and land, and to subscribe to stock, to support road, canal, and waterway improvement projects—and, later, railroads. To "land dealers, town-site promoters, merchants, and settlers," as Paul W. Gates has written, transportation was the key to prosperity. With federal funds, the West could hope to over-leap the barriers of time and distance, obtaining the capital that was so desperately and chronically short in this newest-settled region.[3]

As the region's politicians and editors constantly reminded Congress, "the western states . . . [were] too poor, too exhausted, to engage in those public works," requiring vast sums of capital, with-out the help of their national government.[4] Although they pressed their case on Congress with only mixed success, the states of the Old Northwest nonetheless emerged in the canal era—led by Ohio in the mid-1820s, then with Indiana, Illinois, and Michigan following— as vanguard states for public construction of canal facilities (in Michigan's case, railroads), employing the power of state govern-ment in outright public enterprise. In the 1850s, moreover, the Old Northwest became the scene of the nation's most intensive railroad construction.[5] Thus the history of these western states provides a rich storehouse of material for understanding how American gov-ernmental institutions and American law helped to shape—and in turn were shaped by—the Transportation Revolution.

What follows in this paper is an overview and appraisal of the Transportation Revolution in American law. First, focusing on congressional debates, I shall re-examine the constitutional issues that absorbed politicians and their constituents from about 1815 to the Civil War. Then, the more formal arena of the United States Supreme Court will be examined, to see how constitutional deci-sions interacted with congressional decisions—and with congres-sional abdications of power and responsibility. Finally, a very brief set of suggestions about the interpretation of state law and public policy will be offered, with more detailed data and analysis left to other contributors to this volume in their articles on western canals, railroads, and waterways.

I. THE NATIONAL ARENA

The U.S. Supreme Court has adjudicated most of the great constitutional questions in American history. Even the slavery issue, finally settled on the battlefields of the Civil War, and the constitutional issues concerning the regulatory and welfare state, settled in a sense at the polls, came before the Supreme Court in crucial episodes of their respective histories. Internal improvements as a constitutional issue was different in this regard. From the Republic's earliest days, when there was halting but steady movement in Congress to use federal power for navigational and transport improvement, to the 1850s, when the propriety of railroad land grants was hotly debated, the constitutional issues found expression in congressional proceedings, presidential messages, and the public prints. Only on rare occasions did the basic question before the public— the proper role of the national government in the promotion of transport improvement—find expression in constitutional cases in the courts. The two outstanding Supreme Court cases were *Gibbons* v. *Ogden* in 1824, in which the Court ruled on the commerce clause powers as a limitation on what *the states* might do in controlling the terms of navigation; and the Charles River Bridge Case, which similarly concerned the proper reach of state power, in this instance state power as limited by contract clause rights.[6] Federal aid to internal improvements as a "federalism" issue, concerning the proper allocation of responsibilities as between the national government and the states, was a question no less important in constitutional law than issues concerning contract clause and commerce clause theory. The internal-improvements question found expression and resolution almost exclusively in the political arena, not in the federal courts —but did so as a constitutional, and not merely a policy, question.

The participants in the public debate over federalism and internal improvements addressed basic questions about the nature of republican government. They believed that they were settling important constitutional questions, and this belief accounts for the duration and intensity of the debate. The political leadership of that era did not regard the Supreme Court as having the exclusive responsibility for settling major constitutional issues; Congress and the executive, as they were then seen, shared equally in that responsibility.[7]

Some of the landmarks in the history of federal policy on internal improvements are well known. They include the decisions of Congress in the 1790s to build lighthouses and to establish military and post roads; the Ohio Statehood Act, setting aside 5 percent of the proceeds of public land sales for internal improvements (including 2 percent for the National Road); and authorization in 1806 of the National Road, with construction actually commencing a few years later—the principal Jeffersonian legacy in the field of transportation development. In 1817 President James Madison vetoed the Bonus Bill, which would have set aside a fund for internal improvements derived from revenues from the Bank of the United States, the president insisting that such a plan threatened that quintessential element in the American political system, the "definite partition of powers between the General and State Governments."[8] In 1822 President James Monroe presented Congress with an elaborate, discursive message declaring the necessity for an amendment to the Constitution to authorize spending for internal improvements by the national government. Two years later the General Survey Act was passed, authorizing the Army engineers to conduct surveys. There followed both special land grants to western states in aid of road and canal programs, and subscriptions to the stock of companies such as the Chesapeake and Ohio Canal Company and the Louisville and Portland Canal Company; in addition, there was a rising tide of expenditures for river and harbor improvements, as well as roads, as the annual "pork-barrel" bill became ever more ambitious and complex. Andrew Jackson's attack on the whole system—and its corruption, as he viewed it—with his Maysville Road veto in 1830 established a new ideological orthodoxy for the reigning party. Still, annual expenditures for a variety of projects continued, only to be challenged anew by later Democratic presidents. Despite the use of land grants as alternatives to direct expenditures, as was done for the Illinois Central Railroad and for the Sault Canal project, Jacksonian restraint prevailed on the whole. The debate over constitutionality went on through the 1850s, but the scene of meaningful action had long since passed to the state governments and to the private sector.[9]

Despite this "great parade of constitutional scruples," George Rogers Taylor has written, "the real obstacle which defeated a national system of internal improvements is to be found in the bitter state and sectional jealousies" of that day.[10] The rhetoric of constitutionalism, Taylor and many other analysts contend, was a facade that merely obscured the "real" forces in politics. A reappraisal of the debate in Congress suggests, however, that this sort of "realistic" view of the matter can be overdone. Although the strength of localism and sectionalism cannot be denied, by any means, still constitutional ideologies occasionally transcended considerations of regionalism. At several critical junctures in the course of the debate, moreover, considerations of principle prevailed; and the discipline of the political parties was used to bring the rank and file into line. The most notable example was the Maysville Road veto and the ensuing ideological hardening of Democratic party doctrine.[11]

What was it that the opponents of a federal system of transportation most feared? A remarkable insight can be gained by considering a letter James Madison wrote to Martin Van Buren in 1826. Madison's views reflect the authentically *political* and *ideological* concern—what a friendly critic would have called evidence of Madison's concern for "republican purity"—with which Madison approached the question of internal improvements.[12] "The policy and advantage of roads and canals," Madison wrote, had taken an "extensive and permanent hold of the public will." Hence it was impossible for him to imagine either Congress or the electorate accepting a surrender of congressional authority to appropriate funds for transportation projects. Given this dilemma, Madison averred, it seemed best "to obviate the unconstitutional precedent" —as he regarded the cumulative record of Congress on internal improvements—"by an amendatory article expressly granting the power." If such an amendment were adopted, at least then Congress's exercise of power in this area of policy would not appear to be a precedent for other types of action that enlarged the federal government's sphere. Madison readily admitted that Congress had engaged in this usurpation of power "with the approbation of their constituents"; it was not a situation comparable to that of the Alien and Sedition Acts in 1798, when Congress had thwarted the will of the people.[13]

Madison's conclusion that a constitutional amendment should

be adopted was not in itself extraordinary; he had suggested its advisability years earlier, when he was president, and both Thomas Jefferson and Monroe had similarly given public approval to an amendment of some kind. What made Madison's view in 1826 truly remarkable was that he linked his wish for a constitutional amendment with a proposal that the Constitution's general welfare clause be scrapped.[14] Madison wrote that while the phrase

> 'common defense & general welfare' remain in the Constitution unguarded against the construction which has been contended for, a fund of power inexhaustible, and wholly subversive of the equilibrium between the General and the State Governments is within the reach of the former. Why then not precede all other amendments by one, expunging the phrase, which is not required for any harmless meaning; or making it harmless, by annexing to it, the terms 'in the cases authorized by this Constitution.'[15]

As this passage clearly indicates, Madison regarded the Hamiltonian "broad-constructionist" version of the general welfare clause as being part and parcel of the problem represented more proximately by the popular pressure for federal construction of roads and canals. A formal amendment to the Constitution, he believed, was the way to slip the knot; otherwise, abuse of what he regarded as proper constitutional limitations on national power would become a commonplace thing—the people would become insensitive to the danger.

In the halls of Congress, too, the fear of centralized power as the result of aid to internal improvements found vivid expression. The 1820 census, giving enlarged representation to the West, led immediately to increased pressure for river and harbor appropriations, for subscriptions to canal companies' stock, and for two types of aid specifically aimed at meeting the needs of the newer western states: appropriations for repair, construction, and collection of tolls on the National Road (which was not built even into Ohio until 1825), and grants of land from the federal public domain in aid of western state canal and road projects.[16] Prior to 1820, Madison's own principled opposition, while president, to the Bonus Bill dedication of national revenues for road and canal construction, and, before that, the exigencies of war and the vast rise in public debt resulting from the war with England, had successfully impeded efforts to pry loose national funds for internal improvements. Madison's concern in 1826 that consolidated, centralized power was jeopardizing the integrity of the Republic reflected the sharp turnabout that occurred in the early 1820s. To many besides Madison, it seemed that the floodgates had opened. President John Quincy Adams kept Congress under pressure to recognize a legitimate national responsibility in the area of internal improvements; the newly augmented representation in Congress from the West proved to be a fairly cohesive bloc in voting on internal improvements; and, perhaps most ominously of all, vote-trading and coalition formation seemed to generate an ever-rising flood of demands for federal aid—aid not only to the West, but also to such eastern projects as the Chesapeake and Delaware Canal Company and the Chesapeake and Ohio Canal Company.[17]

Emblematic of the western position in the debates of the 1820s was Senator William Hendricks of Indiana. He was first elected to the Senate in 1824, after having served as governor of Indiana; he

Indiana Historical Society Library

Early National Road scene

remained a senator for twelve years.[18] Hendricks was a prominent figure in nearly all the major debates on federal aid during that time, consistently aligning himself in favor of policies for positive action. He followed the example of Henry Clay, who in 1824 had tried to establish a pragmatic position on the issue, contending that, so long as "forebearance, liberality, practical good sense, and mutual concession" were brought into play, the citizenry had little reason to fear centralization of power. "All the dreaded conflicts of authorities [in the federal system] will be found to be perfectly imaginary," Clay had argued, if only the opponents of the National Road and other forms of federal aid would yield a bit and show generosity.[19] Insofar as he could, Clay avoided admitting that constitutional issues involving basic principle were at stake when internal-improvements policy was debated. Similarly with Hendricks: in 1828, when a bill was before the Senate for the appropriation of funds to repair the National Road and extend it farther west, Hendricks insisted it was too late in the day to raise constitutional objections. It was self-evident, Hendricks declared, that the road was a project of national importance; it was equally self-evident that Congress had the power to act.[20] As Clay so often argued, moreover, Hendricks averred that it was of paramount importance to foster projects that united "the feelings and interests of the East and the West"—an objective "far more important than all the millions which could possibly be expended" on the National Road or similar undertakings.[21] Demonstrating his willingness to see federal largess given wherever it was of manifest benefit, or perhaps merely demonstrating his vote-trading ingenuity, Hendricks emerged in 1829–1830 as a strong advocate of bills to appropriate surveys for a trans-Florida canal, a road to link Memphis with Little Rock, and other projects not directly of benefit to his own section or state.[22]

Meanwhile, Hendricks gave his support to policies that might relieve the West of its dependence on federal appropriations; above all, he contended that "the Federal Government had no constitutional power to hold the soil of the States"—except, of course, to build national roads, fortifications, and other facilities—and so he sponsored bills to graduate the price of public lands and to cede grants of federal land within their borders to the individual states.[23]

In counterpoint with this type of pragmatic appeal for a "sensible" use of national powers, the western representatives in the 1820s demanded aid as a matter of equity. So far as the National Road was concerned, Hendricks and his colleague Senator James Noble declared, a sacred compact was the source of Congress's obligation to provide funds: Ohio and the other western states had agreed to tax exemptions for federal lands for five years after their sale, in exchange for the certainty that the National Road would be constructed.[24] "Will you," Noble asked, "after making a compact, refuse to do what you promised to those States who have been struggling for years in the forest, extending your dominions, and guarding your frontiers against the depredations of the savages?"[25]

William Henry Harrison echoed the triple theme developed by Clay and Hendricks, advocating a pragmatic view of federal authority and the propriety of congressional expenditures, stressing that a sacred compact had been made with the West, and demanding that Congress help to improve conditions in the newly settled regions as a matter of equity: "He [Harrison] did not think it necessary to argue the constitutional question, which he agreed with his colleague had long since been settled." As to the costs of the National Road and similar projects, "the advantages are equal to the expenditure."[26] Harrison pursued a similar line of argument when he led the fight in 1827–1828 for a grant of land to aid the Ohio Canal and Miami Canal projects, on which the state of Ohio had embarked. He stated there was ample precedent for grants of land to western states, so that constitutionality should not be an issue; and aid to the West, he argued, was a simple matter of equity—for the government had obtained the land from the Indians at less than a penny an acre, while the sweat and toil of the early settlers had made those lands worth $1.25 an acre or more. The beneficial effects of interregional transportation improvement, moreover, would be of national scope. The West, Harrison declared, "had only asked what would greatly benefit the United States, and for which the Government ought to pay its share."[27]

Earlier in the decade, before the reapportionment that followed the 1820 census shifted the tide of power, one of the western senators had written in some despair, following defeat of a bill to grant lands to Ohio to aid canal construction: "From the south and even from the east there is a strong jealousy of the rising prosperity of the northwest. We must rely on our own resources. We have little to expect from Congress."[28] By 1825, with the General Survey

Act providing funds for surveys by the Army engineers of improvements projects deemed of national importance now approved and in operation and with other successes being registered by advocates of federal aid, western congressmen could say that "western views" had been advanced considerably.[29] The leadership of the western bloc—Clay, Hendricks, Harrison, and Thomas Hart Benton—by decade's end had enjoyed success in obtaining passage of bills for major land grants to Ohio, Indiana, and Illinois for canals, a small grant to Ohio for a road project, federal subscriptions to the stock of the Louisville and Portland Canal Company, and substantial appropriations for Great Lakes harbor improvements and for western river improvements.[30]

As I indicated earlier, it would be misleading to see this record of western legislative victories as evidence only of sectionalism. On the one hand, several major eastern projects for canals and roads, as well as eastern harbor improvements, also won congressional support in the 1820s. On the other hand, the seriousness with which Clay, Hendricks, and others had to address constitutional questions reminds us that basic principle was in the forefront of debate. Their opponents never let them deny the relevance of basic principle; it could have been said aptly of their debates as John Marshall said of the issues in *McCulloch* v. *Maryland*: "We must never forget that it is a *constitution* we are expounding." Moreover, the result of these debates did affect profoundly the nature of the working Constitution.

We have already seen how former President Madison sought by amending the Constitution to minimize the damage (as he viewed it) to constitutional principle already done by 1826. There were others, including western congressmen, who did not necessarily believe that a doctrinal catastrophe had occurred—who did not view the Republic as being in mortal danger—yet who occupied the sort of middle ground that Madison advocated. Champions of federal aid to internal improvements, they looked for constitutional formulae that could blunt the edge of sectional, ideological, and partisan conflict. Senator Thomas Hart Benton, for example, proposed in 1828 a series of resolutions pointing toward cession of the National Road to the states through which it passed. He favored federal "power to make roads and canals of national importance," Benton declared, "but he could not give . . . his adhesion to the cause which the ultras of the party seemed to demand, namely, a blind and fanatical support of every bill, no matter how got up, or how got in, which had the word 'road' or 'canal' in it."[31] Echoes of this sort of initiative were to be heard in later years, as in the "surplus distribution" scheme of the mid-1830s (turning over surplus federal revenues to the states, in an early-day revenue sharing experiment) or in President James K. Polk's and Stephen A. Douglas's plans to aid state transportation projects by allocating federal tonnage duties to them for that purpose.[32]

More immediately, however, the advocates of internal improvements—from the East as well as the West—faced the unyielding principled opposition of those who thought that even constitutional amendment was unacceptable. As one scholar has summarized their view, "They loved individual liberty, they feared government, and they feared the Federal government more than state and local government."[33] Thus Congressman Andrew Stevenson of Virginia declared, in the debate on the 1824 General Survey Act, that "he loved the West, but he loved the Constitution and the interests of his country more." He warned that to permit federal aid to be given "would be the apple of discord and disunion," instead of promoting interregional harmony and common interest.[34] Stevenson was still willing, in 1824, to contemplate a constitutional amendment on the lines Madison would later propose. Within a few years, however, he had hardened in his opposition. Reacting to the spate of new appropriations in the late 1820s, Stevenson warned that involving the national government in a host of local and state projects would bring "the utter destruction of all the land marks between the powers of the two Governments." The federal system, as the founders had intended it to operate, would be destroyed. If pressed so incessantly, the demand for aid to internal improvements would reduce Congress to the status of "a diet for local and geographical objects, which in time would be made subservient to political views, and to ambitious and designing men . . . leading to the keenest excitements of faction and party and finally, he feared, to corruption."[35]

Others came back to the theme of incipient corruption. Thus Senator William Smith of South Carolina, in the 1828 debates on the general appropriations for river and harbor improvements, deplored the notion that one state or another should be entitled to largess because it wished to make itself more attractive to settlement.

He cited a petition of Indiana asking for federal aid for roads, canals, and bridges, stating that this would permit the state's population to increase and prosper. "What motive can the Government of the United States have," he asked indignantly, "for increasing the population of Indiana, more than that of any other State?"[36] If this sort of appeal should be honored, he warned, "it must bankrupt this Government, and introduce a species of corruption that would taint it to its vitals." The system of federal aid for state and local projects, Smith said, was nothing but "a system . . . of buying the People with their own money."[37] Smith deplored, too, the resort of internal improvements advocates to use of the term "national" to describe major transport projects. The word "national" itself, he said, "had crept into our political vocabulary. . . . It was a term unknown to the origin and theory of our Government."[38]

Similarly, Senator Nathaniel Macon of North Carolina declared that "the Constitution was dead and gone" already, given the role the federal government was already playing. "The more you stretch the Constitution," he warned, "the more you create heart-burnings among the different States; because the People never will believe that they are treated alike; and they can't be, in a country so large as this is."[39] That the doctrine of implied powers, subscribed to by the advocates of federal aid to internal improvements, was a threat for reasons that transcended the issue of roads and canals alone, also became evident. Thus Smith of South Carolina warned that broad construction, in constitutional interpretation, had produced "your Sedition Laws, Tariffs, Colonization Societies, Memorials for a General Emancipation" and the like.[40] And in the General Survey Act debate, John Randolph of Virginia said flatly that the premises on which that bill was founded would equally justify federal action "[to] emancipate every slave in the United States."[41]

Whatever the relative force of ideological conviction on the one side, and sectional self-interest on the other, in the debates of the 1820s it was ideology that had the most enduring effect over the next thirty years, to the eve of the Civil War. This was so because Andrew Jackson elevated the fear of corruption to the status of immutable Democratic party orthodoxy. Both in his Maysville Road veto message—condemning the practice of giving federal support to a local road, lying within a single state—and in his more general pronouncements on the issue—Jackson enshrined the views of Old Republicans such as Macon and Randolph: to open the public trough to a host of local interests, Jackson feared, was to risk the fundamental corruption of republican institutions.[42] As so often happens, moreover, the disciples proved more orthodox than the prophet. Whereas Jackson continued to exercise his own judgment, as chief executive, in approving annual appropriations for river and harbor improvements that he deemed "national" rather than "local," his Democratic successors—from Martin Van Buren to James Buchanan—took a much harder line; so, too, did many of his followers in Congress, who kept up an unremitting attack against expansion of federal aid. The result was a record of reduced federal aid in the late 1830s, additional presidential vetoes in later years, and a crippling lack of continuity in internal-improvements policy. By the fifties, it could fairly be said, there was no policy worthy of the name; the center of initiative was no longer in Washington.[43]

How constitutional debate had reached a deadlock was illustrated by an episode in the Congress in the 1847–1848 session, when President Polk's veto of a river and harbor bill in the previous session was given a full airing. Nearly all the arguments on both sides were much the same as had been heard in congressional halls a quarter century earlier. Caleb B. Smith of Indiana favored new appropriations, arguing that the federal power was "settled clearly and conclusively" by earlier precedents; he was answered immediately by congressmen, especially from the South, who denied that precedent justified federal aid; others followed Polk's lead in condemning any system that led to repeated raids on the federal treasury, encouraging speculation, log-rolling, and corruption; others—from Missouri and Illinois, not only the Old South—warned of the dangers of consolidated national power and denounced the idea that "implied powers" legitimately justified federal action. Tennessee, Pennsylvania, Indiana, and Illinois representatives supported resolutions declaring that Congress had a responsibility and unquestioned authority to make appropriations for transportation.[44] The familiar script played itself out quickly, however, for the votes could not be mustered to overturn Polk's veto. When the Illinois Central land grant was approved two years later, it marked the last occasion until the Civil War when Congress would provide significant federal initiative in directing transportation development.[45]

II. THE SUPREME COURT AND FORMAL LAW

While Congress struggled over the years with the issues of federalism and internal improvements, the Supreme Court was largely playing an indirect and subsidiary role. Nonetheless, some of the Court's decisions were noteworthy because they opened the door to activism by the state governments—or else because they did settle positively and more directly at least some secondary constitutional questions relating to the Transportation Revolution. The 1824 decision of *Gibbons* v. *Ogden* is well remembered because it asserted a broad view of the commerce clause. Even in that decision, however, Chief Justice Marshall acknowledged that the states retained authority under the police power to enact inspection, quarantine, and other laws that could have an effect on commerce.[46] Five years later, Marshall's Court formulated the important doctrine of dormant commerce power in *Willson* v. *Blackbird Creek Marsh Company*, when the Court upheld the power of the state of Delaware to authorize a dam that interfered with navigation on a small tidewater creek. So long as Congress had not acted, the Court found, the state was free to pursue other legitimate policy goals—in this instance, the improvement of marsh lands—at the expense of navigation.[47] The Roger B. Taney Court, in subsequent years, elaborated this concept further by developing the theory of concurrent powers under the commerce clause.[48] The net effect of these decisions was to establish the firm constitutional foundation that the state governments needed both for outright public enterprise and for approval of franchises in transport improvement. No decision of the antebellum era more decisively supported state power in the definition of franchise rights than the Charles River Bridge Case of 1837. In that decision, Taney narrowed enormously the potential contract clause limitations upon state government in dealing with chartered companies. Although the charter rights of a bridge company were at issue in this case, Taney explicitly buttressed his opinion by referring to "the millions of property which have been invested in railroads and canals." The states, he declared, must be permitted "to avail themselves of the lights of modern science, and to partake of the benefit of those improvements which are now adding to the wealth and prosperity, and the convenience and comfort of every other part of the civilized world."[49]

Just as the Charles River Bridge decision was critical to the states as they moved toward franchising corporations for a broad range of activities in transportation, so was the 1848 decision in *West River Bridge* v. *Dix* crucial in validating the discretionary authority of the state governments in taking private property for public purposes, including transport lines. This power of eminent domain, the Court ruled in a sweeping decision, "is . . . paramount to all private rights vested under the government, and these last . . . must yield in every instance to its proper exercise."[50] Again, in this instance, the Court made clear that property rights were not immutable; the pathways must be cleared for enterprise, public and private, and the state legislatures and courts were to be given a virtually free hand in determining when older forms of property rights must be sacrificed in the quest for material progress.[51] Two years later, in *Mills* v. *St. Clair County*, the Supreme Court indicated how completely it had retreated from older vested-rights doctrines. In this instance, the state of Illinois had taken both the land and the franchise rights of a ferry owner, under eminent domain, and transferred them to another ferry operator. Although the Supreme Court acknowledged that there had been an obvious injustice since inadequate compensation had been paid, it was exclusively the Illinois government's responsibility and not a question for federal courts' review.[52] In 1852, moreover, the Court held that despite the ruling in *Gibbons*, a state had the power to establish a navigational monopoly of a purely intrastate character; and in 1855 the Court validated regulation of coastal fisheries by the states, against commerce clause claims.[53]

The constitutional status of inland waterways—an issue vital to western interests—became a prominent subject of both congressional attention and Supreme Court action in the years immediately following the 1839–1843 depression. The mid-forties inaugurated what I have termed elsewhere the distinct "second phase" of the Transportation Revolution. This phase was marked, first of all, by the proliferation of transport lines in the West, with major new canal lines linking the Great Lakes and Mississippi River basins completed in Pennsylvania, Ohio, Indiana, and Illinois. Second, it was marked by a vast increase of tonnage and traffic on the western rivers, with as much steamer tonnage built during 1836–1842 as had been constructed in the entire period before 1836, with a continuing strength of flatboat traffic and a sharp rise in Great Lakes tonnage.

Third, the opening of so many competing routes by 1848, together with the expansion of steamer capacity and, by 1850, railroad traffic as well, produced a sharp decline in freight rates.[54]

Given this magnitude and rapidity of change, it is not surprising that Congress and the federal courts should have reconsidered the long-standing constitutional doctrine that held that inland waterways, beyond the ocean tide's ebb and flow, were not subject to federal maritime or admiralty jurisdiction.[55] Especially from the mercantile communities of the Great Lakes and river cities came petitions and complaints asking Congress to extend federal maritime jurisdiction to inland navigable waters. Otherwise, a crippling confusion would prevail in settling tort suits and other legal cases, which invariably raised difficult questions as to which state or states properly had jurisdiction when shippers, shipowners, passengers, and other litigants were from different states of residence and the commerce was interstate and interregional, along far-flung networks. A typical petition was from residents of the city of Chicago and of St. Joseph, Michigan, in 1843, averring that

> much inconvenience has been experienced by those engaged in the commerce, shipping and navigation of the Northern Chain of Lakes, in consequence of the want of any general laws and provisions of Congress regulating the same. . . . Your petitioners would represent that the navigation of the Lakes, the nature of the perils and the length of the voyages thereon, the character of the shipping and the contracts growing out of such navigation, are similar, in most respects, to those of the high seas and especially, to those of the coasting trade, now under the regulations and subject to the maritime law of the United States.[56]

Many leading legal authorities deplored the lack of uniformity and federal jurisdiction, lending the weight of their prestige to demands for reform.[57] To spokesmen for reform, it seemed absurd to leave to the confusion and conflict of competing state jurisdictions the commerce of the interior on sole grounds that "God, in His wisdom, did not cause salt water instead of fresh to fill these Great Lakes, and create a tide that would ebb and flow upon them."[58]

Stephen A. Douglas liked to take credit for the reform movement's success, which produced in 1845 an act extending the jurisdiction of federal district courts to cover most of the commercial navigation on inland waters.[59] In fact, however, Justice Joseph Story was the key figure in the enactment of the new law; he drew up the legislation, it seems, and threw his prestige behind it.[60] The congressional debate reflected strong western sentiment—though not without prominent exceptions, most notably the respected one-time Ohio jurist Benjamin Tappan, who opposed this extension of national power as unnecessary—but also drew upon considerable support from other regions.[61]

The validity of the congressional initiative was soon tested, as the Supreme Court was called upon to examine a constitutional challenge to the 1845 law. To uphold the law would require the Court to overrule its own decision of many years standing that defined navigable waters and hence federal jurisdiction by the ebb and flow of tides, the old English rule. In a decision by the chief justice, the Court candidly acknowledged the "growing commerce on the lakes and navigable rivers of the western States" was a factor that weighed heavily in its deliberations on the matter. The Court upheld the new law and renounced its old doctrine, which dated from 1825.[62]

A counterpoint of legislative and judicial power also marked a second issue in constitutional law that was given new urgency by the Transportation Revolution's second phase. This issue concerned jurisdiction over bridges spanning the great rivers of the interior. Again, a doctrine set down by the Supreme Court was the cause of some difficulty: in 1847 Virginia and Ohio had authorized a company to build a bridge spanning the busy Ohio River at Wheeling; then the Supreme Court ruled that the bridge was a public nuisance because it interfered with steamer navigation.[63] Immediately Congress declared the bridge lawful and declared it officially a postal road. Again called upon in 1856 to rule in the case—on complaint of the state of Pennsylvania, which had opposed the bridge from the outset—the Court, with three justices dissenting vigorously, yielded to the wishes of Congress and declared the act constitutional as an exercise of the commerce power.[64]

Taking in sum (a) the formal decisions of the Supreme Court on matters shaping the institutional context of the Transportation Revolution and (b) the policy decisions of Congress that to an even greater degree established the terms of the working Constitution, it is clear that centralizing doctrines of national power were asserted with only partial success. As a practical matter, despite shifts in the locus of real power toward the center, represented by decisions such as the second Wheeling Bridge Case, the working Constitution from Andrew Jackson's presidency until the Civil War was one that left policy initiative and responsibility in transport development mainly to the states.[65]

III. THE STATE ARENAS

In the national forum of political and constitutional debate, the "federalism" issue was the principal focus of controversy: what shall the central government do, and what should be left to the states? In the constitutional conventions, legislatures, and courts of the states, however, controversy centered on such questions as the following: (1) To what degree should state government (and its offspring, local government) take full outright responsibility for internal improvements, and to what degree should initiatives be left to the private sector? (2) What priorities might be formulated and imposed, either to maximize the "rationality" of transport planning, or to maximize "fairness" in the sharing of benefits, or to achieve both ends? (3) How should the state role in outright enterprise or subsidy of private enterprise be financed? (4) What privileges, immunities, and responsibilities might be given to private corporations, chartered to undertake transportation development? and at what costs to those enterprises, and to the government? and (5) To what extent should public law and the common law be reshaped—as in tort law, for example, with its doctrines of fault and liability—to allocate the costs that society (or private individuals and firms) had to bear in some way as the result of transport innovation?

Of course, seldom were such questions formally posed in precisely those terms. When they did find formal expression, it was generally in constitutional conventions, or in litigation on great questions of common law, or in legislative debates at those rare moments—such as Indiana experienced when its canal system became a state commitment in the 1830s—when a major policy decision for authorization of a long-term construction project had to be confronted. More commonly, these questions came before the public, if they surfaced in open discussion at all, as part of the background of debate over a specific area of state policy (such as tax reform) or a specific project within a larger system (a particular railroad charter, for example). Some scholars have argued, in fact, that the legal process typical of the antebellum state governments seldom brought the most important questions explicitly before the public—at least in a form that made potential costs and benefits explicit, or established coherent priorities, or defined administrative needs and externalities in any systematic way.[66]

It is axiomatic that to understand American law in the early nineteenth century, one must keep in the forefront of analysis the fact that "dual federalism" was a reality: each state had its own particular mix of policies; the timing of development and settlement varied, and the variation had an impact on differences among the states; the economic and social milieux of the individual states varied, with effects on policy choices; and, perhaps most important, the states operated in what they openly defined and recognized as a competitive system, in which they pursued essentially "mercantilist" policies designed to acquire capital, settlement, and advantage at the expense (if necessary) of other states in the system.[67]

What follows here is only a set of suggestions as to how the western states, in the era of the Transportation Revolution, shaped their constitutional law, policy, and structure in response to perceived needs of the day. Full and detailed analysis depends upon close examination of specific transport innovations and their histories, as is done in other essays in this volume.

The capacity of state government in providing citizens with transport and the propriety of such state action was a matter that found consistent resolution in Ohio, Indiana, Illinois, and Michigan. In each of those states, from 1825, when Ohio first acted, until the late 1830s, extensive debate, engineering surveys, analysis of alternative technologies, and the compromise of sectional rivalries resulted in commitments to major state programs of transportation. In each state, debt financing was resorted to, on the model of the Erie Canal in New York (and, for the others, of Ohio's successful first-stage canal project of 1825–1834). In each instance, the commitment to a major project, or set of projects, led immediately to the building of a state bureaucracy and incorporation of expertise on a virtually unprecedented scale into the mechanisms for state action. The quality of performance, of course, varied; and the success of those projects that were completed also varied. None of these four states conformed to the model of "drift and default" that is sometimes said to characterize the antebellum states, with little in the way of conscious decision making, public analysis of alternative policies, and the like.[68] In these states, both the engineers charged with designing the works and many of the political leaders who led debates on how to proceed adhered to a concept of planned priorities. They did not always prevail, by any means, but their contributions to debate lent more care and rationality to public discussion than scholars have sometimes allowed was true. In Wisconsin, which came into the Union in a different era from the others, public enterprise was never considered; the costs and failures of the earlier starters served to persuade Wisconsin to build a nearly ironclad prohibition against state enterprise into its first constitution. It was linked, moreover, with stringent provisions against state indebtedness.[69] Wisconsin's alignment, by 1848, in a position against state enterprise was emblematic of a broader change occurring in the West more generally by that time. As private capital became available, disillusionment with public enterprise set in; and, as the coherence of any planning concepts that survived the great depression of 1839–1843 eroded under pressure of localistic interests, the western states followed the national trend and left railroad promotion mainly to private-sector interests.[70]

In all these states, however, there was evidence of contending views of how public policy—whatever the degree of outright public enterprise to be permitted—should be shaped. Planning, as has been noted, was usually advocated by the engineers and an element of state leadership in the legislatures and governors' chairs.[71] A second force, working against planning, was localism—the sort of pressure that an Indiana state engineer despairingly acknowledged when he said in 1835, "Most of the members [of the legislature] vote for nothing which does not pass through their own county."[72] This forced lawmakers and the bureaucracy to shape programs not to serve rational priorities, but "to buy votes."[73] Perhaps the worst case was Illinois, when in 1837 a "mammoth bill" was enacted that seemed to give something to everyone. "At that day," Stephen A. Douglas recalled, "the people were for the system—almost en masse. So strong was the current of popular feeling in its favor that it was hazardous for any politician to oppose it."[74] Much the same situation came to prevail in the other public-enterprise states; overbuilding and overcommitment was the result and, by a piece of colossal bad luck, was linked in time to the century's worst business depression to that date. What survived the debacle that resulted was persistent localism, now charged with loss of faith in the public sector.[75]

Another force in the legal process in the states was principled egalitarianism—the belief that as a matter of right, not merely of expediency, every section of a state ought to have some of the state's largess. In several states the method developed to serve this principle was formula-based "mixed enterprise," in which state subscriptions were made available on a matching basis when locally based promoters invested in an approved project. This movement coincided with the great surge of public investment and the economic crisis, thus leading to even more disillusionment with the active state.[76]

Outright public investment and enterprise comprised the most dramatic sort of state involvement in transport promotion. There was another way, less costly or dramatic, at least in the short run, for the state to subsidize internal improvements. This way involved the devolution of special privileges and immunities. In all the western states, the corporate charter—and, later, the general railroad corporation law—became a major instrument for allocating such indirect subsidies. Bridge companies, canal companies, turnpike corporations, and railroad firms all received the privilege of taking land and other property on payment of compensation, under the state's eminent domain power. Without this privilege, private enterprise in transport was practically impossible.[77] In addition, the courts of the individual states transferred to private corporations the benefit of cost reducing, subsidizing doctrines in eminent domain. These doctrines had been enunciated originally to reduce the costs of state canal construction, road projects, and other public works. They included, above all, the doctrines that state agents or the company were exempt from trespass and other tort liabilities; that when damages were assessed, the supposed "benefits" recaptured by the owner of property taken could be offset against losses, so that often property owners received little or nothing when eminent domain was exercised; and that payment need not be made immediately on taking, or in advance.[78] All these extraordinary privileges, an Indiana decision proclaimed in 1838, were justified because the highest possible public good was at stake: "the advancement of the wealth, prosperity, and character of the state."[79] Tort immunity for private transport companies was also extended liberally by the courts, to cover the operations as well as the construction activities in many instances.[80] After 1850, some of these privileges were reconsidered by state lawmakers; for example, in the Indiana 1852 general railroad law, as in the 1851 Ohio state constitution, offsetting benefits against damages in eminent domain, at least by private companies, were terminated.[81] On the whole, however, these special immunities and privileges amounted to a subsidy for private sector firms that probably exceeded in value explicit tax exemptions. They were reinforced, moreover, by a policy in the 1850s in all the Old Northwest states of permitting various types of local-government aid.[82]

In sum, the entire fabric of American law—including both constitutional doctrine and subnational law, both public and judge-made—was reshaped in response to the demands of the Transportation Revolution. The influence ran, of course, both ways: law also shaped transport development. If the constitutional stalemate that prevented the national government from playing a larger and more influential role had the short-run effect of slowing transport development, it also had the longer-run effect of leading to rivalry and considerable duplication of activity by leaving the initiative to the states. The resultant institutional context of transport policy, featuring states scrambling in a competition to outdo one another in spending and in extending privileges, doubtless had a stimulative effect on the overall level of investment and innovation. In 1834 an Indiana state representative, writing to urge Senator John Tipton to support a bill extending federal aid to a local Indiana project, said: "All States are in the habit of begging!"[83] If that was true in the 1830s, by 1860 it could be said with equal truth that all the Old Northwest states were sovereign; if they begged anywhere, it was only at the financial centers where railroad capital was to be found. Whether they had used their hard-won sovereignty wisely in the development of their internal improvement systems and what the begging had won them, are questions still worth pondering.

NOTES

The author is grateful to the Rockefeller Foundation for a Humanities Fellowship, and to Project '87 for a research grant, in support of research on which this paper is based.

1. *State* v. *Beackmo*, 8 Blackford 246, 250 (Indiana, 1846). Constitutional issues as debated nationally and with regard to specific measures are considered at length in the works of Frederick Jackson Turner, especially his early book, *The Rise of the New West, 1819–1829* (New York: Harper & Brothers, 1906); George Dangerfield, *The Era of Good Feelings* (London: Methuen and Co., 1953); Carter Goodrich, *Government Promotion of American Canals and Railroads, 1800–1890* (New York: Columbia University Press, 1960); Jeremiah S. Young, *A Political and Constitutional Study of the Cumberland Road* (Chicago, 1902); and R. Carlyle Buley, *The Old Northwest: Pioneer Period, 1815–1840* (2 volumes. Indianapolis: Indiana Historical Society, 1950).

The standard work on the promotion, technology, financing, and construction of internal improvements before 1860, as well as on institutional economic change of the period, is George Rogers Taylor, *The Transportation Revolution, 1815–1860* (New York: Rinehart & Co., 1951). See also Harry N. Scheiber and Stephen Salsbury, "Reflections on George Rogers Taylor's *The Transportation Revolution: 1815–1860:* A Twenty-five Year Retrospect," in *Business History Review*, LI (1977), 79–89.

2. Turner, *The Rise of the New West*; Curtis Nettels, "The Mississippi Valley and the Constitution, 1815–29," in *Mississippi Valley Historical Review*, XI (1924–1925), 332–57; Philip D. Jordan, *The National Road* (Indianapolis: Bobbs-Merrill Co., 1948), pp. 159–76 *passim*. The issue can be viewed profitably from the perspective of one prominent national leader's career in the biography by Robert W. Johannsen, *Stephen A. Douglas* (New York: Oxford University Press, 1973).

3. The quotation is from Paul W. Gates, "Introduction," in Nellie A. Robertson and Dorothy Riker (eds.), *The John Tipton Papers* (3 volumes. *Indiana Historical Collections*, XXIV, XXV, and XXVI, Indianapolis: Indiana Historical Bureau, 1942), I, 12.

4. Cincinnati *Liberty Hall and Cincinnati Gazette*, February 6, 1824.

5. The literature on the Transportation Revolution in the West is amply cited in the other studies in this volume.

6. *Gibbons* v. *Ogden*, 9 Wheaton 1 (1824); *Proprietors of Charles River Bridge* v. *Proprietors of Warren Bridge*, 11 Peters 420 (1837). Compare with Harry N. Scheiber, "Federalism and the American Economic Order, 1789–1910," in *Law & Society Review*, X (1975), 58–83.

7. Compare with Donald G. Morgan, *Congress and the Constitution: A Study of Responsibility* (Cambridge, Mass.: Belknap Press of Harvard University Press, 1966), pp. 112–21.

8. Monroe's message, May 4, 1822, in *Annals of Congress*, 17 Cong., 1 Sess., 1809–63.

9. Goodrich, *Government Promotion of American Canals and Railroads*; Paul Wallace Gates, *History of Public Land Law Development* (Washington, D.C.: U.S. Government Printing Office, 1968), pp. 319–86; Ralph D. Gray, *The Great National Waterway: A History of the Chesapeake & Delaware Canal, 1769–1965* (Urbana: University of Illinois Press, 1967); John Bell

Rae, "Federal Land Grants in Aid of Canals," in *Journal of Economic History*, IV (1944), 167–77; John N. Dickinson, *To Build a Canal: Sault Ste. Marie, 1853–1854 and After* (Columbus: Miami-Ohio State University Press, 1981); Johannsen, *Stephen A. Douglas*; Forest G. Hill, *Roads, Rails and Waterways* (Norman: University of Oklahoma Press, 1957).

10. Taylor, *The Transportation Revolution*, pp. 20–21.

11. James D. Richardson (comp.), *A Compilation of the Messages and Papers of the Presidents, 1789–1897* (Washington, D.C.: Government Printing Office, 1897), II, 1046.

12. James Madison to Martin Van Buren, Montpelier, Virginia, September 20, 1826, Van Buren Papers, Manuscript Division, Library of Congress.

13. *Ibid.*

14. Although Chief Justice Marshall denied, in private correspondence, the validity of Alexander Hamilton's view that "the words 'to pay the debts and provide for the common defense and general welfare of the United States' were to be considered as a substantive grant of power," the sentiment was frequently expressed in Congress that Hamilton's view was correct; in any event, Marshall's own doctrine, especially as enunciated in *McCulloch* v. *Maryland*, 4 Wheaton 421 (1819), as to the sweep of the "necessary and proper" clause was equally worrisome to spokesmen for the limited-powers view. Marshall to Timothy Pickering, March 18, 1828, quoted in Robert K. Faulkner, *The Jurisprudence of John Marshall* (Princeton, N.J.: Princeton University Press, 1968), p. 80. For a contemporary polemical exchange vividly illustrating the fears of despotism inspired by the Hamilton and Marshall doctrines see Gerald Gunther (ed.), *John Marshall's Defense of McCulloch* v. *Maryland* (Stanford, Calif.: Stanford University Press, 1969).

15. Madison to Van Buren, September 20, 1826, Van Buren Papers.

16. Nettels, "The Mississippi Valley and the Constitution, 1815–29," in *Mississippi Valley Historical Review*, XI, 346ff.; Jordan, *The National Road*, pp. 69ff.; Samuel Flagg Bemis, *John Quincy Adams and the Union* (New York: Knopf, 1956), pp. 62ff., 74ff.

17. See works cited in note 9, above.

18. For information on Hendricks see Frederick D. Hill, "William Hendricks: Indiana Politician and Western Advocate, 1812–1850" (Ph.D dissertation, Indiana University, 1972); also Nina Kathleen Reid, "Sketches of Early Indiana Senators—(III) William Hendricks, 1825–1837," in *Indiana Magazine of History*, IX (1913), 167–86.

19. *Annals of Congress*, 18 Cong., 1 Sess., 1030. As early as 1806, when the National Road bill was first approved, Clay had denied the validity of Jefferson's principled view that the national government could lay out the road and take property only by permission of the states. The United States government, he insisted, had the power "to fell the oak of the mountain, to gather the stone which has slept for centuries useless in its bosom," so long as compensation was paid. Quoted in Young, *Cumberland Road*, p. 42.

20. *Congressional Debates*, 20 Cong., 1 Sess., 117. He did not "suppose that it would be necessary, or that the Senate were disposed," Hendricks said, "to

go into an argument on the principles of the [National Road] bill" as Congress's obligation (and power) "had been fully established on former occasions." *Ibid.*, 102.

21. *Ibid.*, 793.

22. *Ibid.*, 21 Cong., 1 Sess., 247, 340–44; *ibid.*, 21 Cong., 2 Sess., 334. Hendricks was also a leading spokesman for federal subscriptions to the Louisville & Portland Canal Company, a project that was, of course, of direct interest to Indiana.

23. *Ibid.*, 20 Cong., 1 Sess., 15–16.

24. *Ibid.*, 117, 122.

25. *Ibid.*, 122.

26. *Ibid.*, 104.

27. *Ibid.*, 19 Cong., 2 Sess., 312–13, 318.

28. William A. Trimble to Ethan A. Brown, April 29, 1820, Ethan Allen Brown Papers, Ohio Historical Society.

29. Benjamin Ruggles to Charles Hammond, May 23, 1824, Charles Hammond Papers, Ohio Historical Society.

30. Harry N. Scheiber, "State Policy and the Public Domain: The Ohio Canal Lands," in *Journal of Economic History*, XXV (1965), 86–113; Paul B. Trescott, "The Louisville and Portland Canal Company, 1825-1874," in *Mississippi Valley Historical Review*, XLIV (1957-1958), 686–708; Hill, *Roads, Rails and Waterways*; Erik F. Haites, James Mak, and Gary M. Walton, *Western River Transportation: The Era of Internal Development, 1810-1860* (Baltimore: Johns Hopkins University Press, 1975).

31. *Congressional Debates*, 20 Cong., 1 Sess., 717–18.

32. Taylor, *The Transportation Revolution*, pp. 357–58; Stephen A. Douglas to Joel A. Matteson, January 2, 1854, in Robert W. Johannsen (ed.), *The Letters of Stephen A. Douglas* (Urbana: University of Illinois Press, 1961), pp. 276–81.

33. Charles S. Sydnor, *The Development of Southern Sectionalism, 1819–1848* (Baton Rouge: Louisiana State University Press, 1948), p. 136.

34. *Annals of Congress*, 18 Cong., 1 Sess., 1264–66.

35. *Ibid.*, 1265; *Congressional Debates*, 20 Cong., 2 Sess., 303, 306–307.

36. *Congressional Debates*, 20 Cong., 1 Sess., 636.

37. *Ibid.*, 639.

38. *Ibid.*, 645.

39. *Ibid.*, 106.

40. *Ibid.*, 651.

41. Quoted in Sydnor, *The Development of Southern Sectionalism*, p. 139.

42. See Taylor, *The Transportation Revolution*, p. 20; Goodrich, *Government Promotion of American Canals and Railroads*, p. 41. In his December, 1830, message, Jackson further pursued the theme of federal aid as a corrupting influence. A House committee, formed to consider this portion of the message, responded forthrightly that some inequalities of distribution were inevitable. The committee offered a logical way around this dilemma with a formula perhaps more artistic than persuasive: "As internal improvements are

the only objects of magnitude alike advantageous to the new States and to the Union, it is by acting on these alone that Congress can equalise the public benefits of the country. . . ." *House Reports*, 21 Cong., 2 Sess., No. 77, pp. 10–11

43. Goodrich, *Government Promotion of American Canals and Railroads*, pp. 41–48; Glyndon Van Deusen, *The Jacksonian Era, 1828–1848* (New York: Harper & Brothers, 1959).

44. *Congressional Globe*, 30 Cong., 1 Sess., 16–17, 29, 33–34, 894, 918.

45. The story of the Illinois Central grant, a political affair of byzantine complexity, is given in Paul Wallace Gates, *The Illinois Central Rail-road and Its Colonization Work* (Cambridge, Mass.: Harvard University Press, 1934), and Johannsen, *Stephen A. Douglas*, pp. 304–17.

46. 9 Wheaton 1 (1824). An important scholarly reconsideration of this case, in the context of mid-1820s debates such as we have studied in the previous section of this article, is provided by W. Howard Mann in "The Marshall Court: Nationalization of Private Rights and Personal Liberty from the Authority of the Commerce Clause," in *Indiana Law Journal*, XXXVIII (1962–1963), 117–238.

47. 2 Peters 245 (1829).

48. See Maurice Baxter, *Daniel Webster & the Supreme Court* (Amherst: University of Massachusetts Press, 1966); Kent Newmyer, "History over Law: The Taney Court," in *Stanford Law Review*, XXVII (1975), 1373ff.

49. 11 Peters 420 (1837). See Stanley I. Kutler, *Privilege and Creative Destruction: The Charles River Bridge Case* (Philadelphia: Lippincott, 1971).

50. 6 Howard 507 (1848). See discussion in Harry N. Scheiber, "The Road to *Munn*: Eminent Domain and the Concept of Public Purpose in the State Courts," in *Perspectives in American History*, V (1971), 378–81.

51. This is a main theme in the overview of American law by James Willard Hurst, *Law and the Conditions of Freedom in the Nineteenth-Century United States* (Madison: University of Wisconsin Press, 1956). See also Harry N. Scheiber, "Property Law, Expropriation, and Resource Allocation by Government: The United States, 1789–1910," in *Journal of Economic History*, XXXIII (1973), 232–51.

52. 8 Howard 569 (1850).

53. *Veazie* v. *Moor*, 14 Howard 567 (1852); *Smith* v. *Maryland*, 18 Howard 71 (1855).

54. Harry N. Scheiber, *Ohio Canal Era: A Case Study of Government and the Economy, 1820–1861* (Athens: Ohio University Press, 1969), pp. 212–14.

55. The doctrine had been set down in *The Steamboat Thomas Jefferson*, 10 Wheaton 428 (1825). See the contemporary commentary by Timothy Walker, "The Project of Extending Admiralty Jurisdiction over the Lakes and Rivers," in *Western Law Journal*, II (1845), 563ff.

56. The petition quoted was dated December 8, 1843, from Chicago, and

an identical one came from St. Joseph. Quoted in Carl B. Swisher, *The Taney Period, 1836–1864* (New York: Macmillan, 1974), p. 428.

57. *Ibid.*, pp. 442–43; Alfred Conkling, *A Treatise on the Organization and Jurisdiction of the Supreme, Circuit and District Courts of the United States* (New York: Gould, Banks & Co., 1842); Milton Conover, "The Abandonment of the 'Tidewater' Concept of Admiralty Jurisdiction in the United States," in *Oregon Law Review*, XXXVIII (1958), 46–48.

58. James L. Barton, *Commerce of the Lakes* (Buffalo, N.Y.: Jewett, Thomas & Co., 1847), quoted in "From Judicial Grant to Legislative Power: The Admiralty Clause in the 19th Century," in *Harvard Law Review*, LXVII (1954), 1221.

59. U.S. *Statutes at Large*, V, 726. Douglas makes his claim in his manuscript "Autobiographical Notes (1859?)," in Johannsen (ed.), *Letters of Stephen A. Douglas*, p. 472.

60. "From Judicial Grant to Legislative Power," in *Harvard Law Review*, LXVII, 1222–23 and notes; Swisher, *The Taney Period*, pp. 429–31, 437, 443. Ironically, Story had written the opinion of the Court in the 1825 case (cited note 55, above), which in a sense was the source of all the trouble!

61. Swisher, *The Taney Period*, pp. 427–31; Conover, "The Abandonment of the 'Tidewater' Concept of Admiralty Jurisdiction in the United States," in *Oregon Law Review*, XXXVIII, 50–51.

62. *The Propeller Genesee Chief v. Fitzhugh*, 12 Howard 443 (1852).

63. *Pennsylvania v. Wheeling Bridge*, 9 Howard 647 (1851); Swisher, *The Taney Period*, pp. 408–18.

64. U.S. *Statutes at Large*, X, 112; *Pennsylvania v. Wheeling Bridge*, 18 Howard 421 (1856). The 1852 law marked the first time, a leading newspaper noted, that Congress had interposed legislative power specifically to overturn a ruling of the Supreme Court. New York *Daily Tribune*, February 19, 1856, cited in Swisher, *The Taney Period*, p. 416. For controversies further embroiling the Supreme Court in navigation issues on western waters see Scheiber, "The Road to *Munn*," in *Perspectives in American History*, V, 349–55.

65. Harry N. Scheiber, "American Federalism and the Diffusion of Power: Historical and Contemporary Perspectives," in *University of Toledo Law Review*, IX (1978), 628–36; Scheiber, "Federalism and the American Economic Order," in *Law & Society Review*, X, 58ff., 86–100. It should be noted that Congress did take one major initiative in regulatory policy—enactment in 1838, then re-enactment in 1852 on a much more effective basis, of safety requirements for steamboat construction and operation on inland waters.

66. Hurst, *Law and the Conditions of Freedom*, chap. 1. Commentary on this important theme is provided in Richard N. Current, "Willard Hurst as Wisconsin Historian," in *Wisconsin Law Review* (1980), pp. 1222–26; and Harry N. Scheiber, "At the Borderland of Law and Economic History," in *American Historical Review*, LXXV (1970), 744–56.

67. Taylor, *The Transportation Revolution*, pp. 378–83; Louis Hartz, *Economic Policy and Democratic Thought: Pennsylvania, 1776–1860* (Cambridge, Mass.: Harvard University Press, 1948); Scheiber, *Ohio Canal Era*, pp. 88 94, 353 65; Ronald E. Shaw, *Erie Water West: A History of the Erie Canal, 1792–1854* (Lexington: University of Kentucky Press, 1966).

68. See note 66, above. Intensive analysis of the Ohio case is in Scheiber, *Ohio Canal Era*.

69. Ray A. Brown, "The Making of the Wisconsin Constitution," in *Wisconsin Law Review* (1949), pp. 648–91, (1952), pp. 25–63

70. Goodrich, *Government Promotion of American Canals and Railroads*, pp. 134–52.

71. Harry N. Scheiber, "Urban Rivalry and Internal Improvements in the Old Northwest, 1820–1860," in *Ohio History*, LXXI (1962), reprinted in Harry N. Scheiber (ed.), *The Old Northwest: Studies in Regional History* (Lincoln: University of Nebraska Press, 1969), pp. 249–63.

72. Jesse Williams to M. T. Williams, January 12, 1835, Micajah T. Williams Papers, Ohio Historical Society.

73. J. Williams to M. T. Williams, January 23, 1835, *ibid*. See also John D. Barnhart and Donald F. Carmony, *Indiana: From Frontier to Industrial Commonwealth* (4 volumes. New York: Lewis Historical Publishing Co., 1954), I, 291–92; Paul Fatout, *Indiana Canals* (West Lafayette, Ind.: Purdue University Studies, 1972), pp. 65–75.

74. Douglas, "Autobiographical Sketch (1838)," in Johannsen (ed.), *The Letters of Stephen A. Douglas*, pp. 67–68.

75. Carter Goodrich, "The Revulsion against Internal Improvements," in *Journal of Economic History*, X (1950), 145–51.

76. For a case study of mixed enterprise, under Ohio's 1837 Loan Law, see Harry N. Scheiber, "The Pennsylvania & Ohio Canal: Transport Innovation, Mixed Enterprise, and Urban Commercial Rivalry, 1825–61," in *The Old Northwest*, VI (1980–1981), 105–36. On egalitarian principle, compare with Scheiber, *Ohio Canal Era*, pp. 91–103, 109–13. In Ohio the Board of Public Works explicitly acknowledged that it was widely believed that "benefits conferred shall be coextensive with the burthens imposed," requiring extension of the state program to all districts. *Ibid.*, p. 109.

77. Victor M. Bogle, "Railroad Building in Indiana, 1850–1855," in *Indiana Magazine of History*, LVIII (1962), 211–32. On law and the Ohio railroads, see Scheiber, *Ohio Canal Era*, pp. 275–98.

78. Indiana decisions include *Rubottom* v. *McClure*, 4 Blackford 505 (Indiana 1838), upholding the eminent domain power and right to enter property for canal commissioners; *McIntyre* v. *State*, 5 Blackford 383 (Indiana 1840), upholding the 1836 internal improvements law that provided for offsetting damages with supposed benefits; and *Vanblaricum* v. *State*, 7 Blackford 209 (Indiana 1844), on appraisal of land taken by its value at the time taken. *Rubottom* also ruled out any necessity of prior payment.

79. *Rubottom* v. *McClure*, 4 Blackford 505, 507 (Indiana 1838). The importance more generally of such doctrines is discussed in Harry N. Scheiber,

"Property Law, Expropriation, and Resource Allocation by Government," in *Journal of Economic History*, XXXIII (1973), 232–51.

80. *Kimble* [Trimble?] v. *White Water Valley Canal Company*, Smith 93 (Indiana 1848), 1 Carter 285 (Indiana 1848); *Commissioners of Franklin County* v. *White Water Valley Canal Company*, 2 Carter 162 (Indiana 1850).

81. *McMahon* v. *The Cincinnati and Chicago Short-line Railroad Company*, 5 Porter 413 (Indiana 1854).

82. Carter Goodrich, "Local Government Planning of Internal Improvements," in *Political Science Quarterly*, LXVI (1951), 411–45.

83. David Guard to John Tipton, January 13, 1834, quoted in Fatout, "Canalling in the Whitewater Valley," in *Indiana Magazine of History*, LX (1964), 51.

Internal Improvements in National Politics, 1816–1830

Douglas E. Clanin

An examination of how political forces in the United States dealt with the issue of federally sponsored internal improvement projects in the fifteen years following the end of the War of 1812 helps to provide clues for an explanation of why an integrated federal program for transportation development was thwarted after President Andrew Jackson's Maysville Road veto in 1830 until the passage of the Federal Aid Road Act of 1916.[1] Whereas strict construction of the Constitution generally held sway during President Thomas Jefferson's terms in office, the end of the War of 1812 marked a watershed in the battle between strict and loose constitutional constructionists. As Frederick Jackson Turner has written, the political leaders of this period were "changing their attitudes toward public questions as the economic conditions of their sections changed," and they were "obliged not only to adjust themselves to the interests of the sections which they represented, but also, if they would achieve a national career, to make effective combinations with other sections."[2]

One of the new political realities that emerged after the War of 1812 was the rise of the West into prominence, which was shown most clearly in that section's increased representation in Congress. This increase was caused by two factors: first, several western states

Douglas E. Clanin is an editor at the Indiana Historical Society. This paper was read as a substitute for the paper scheduled to be presented by Harry N. Scheiber, who was unable to be present because of illness. This study is a revised and condensed version of a work that was originally prepared for Professor Robert Nesbit's research seminar at the University of Wisconsin, Madison, in 1969.

were admitted into the Union. Between 1816 and 1821, Indiana, Mississippi, Illinois, Alabama, and Missouri came into the Union, and, when combined with the previously admitted states of the Mississippi Valley (Ohio, Kentucky, Tennessee, and Louisiana), "formed a compact body of territory, united by similar interests. . . ."[3] Second, the 1820 census resulted in a reapportionment of the House of Representatives.[4] From the Fourteenth Congress (1815–1817) to the Eighteenth Congress (1823–1825), the West increased in strength from 26 to 37 percent in the Senate and from 12 to 22 percent in the House.[5] There was little doubt where this western group stood with respect to federally sponsored internal improvement projects in relation to a narrower, strict constructionist view on that subject. For example, between 1823 and 1829, only James K. Polk of Tennessee out of a total of seventy-four western House members was a strict constructionist. And of twenty-nine western senators who served during the same period, only one, Hugh White of Tennessee, was consistently a strict constructionist.[6]

The reasons for western congressmen's unanimity on the internal improvements issue are not difficult to find. After the War of 1812, western settlers were confronted with a sparsely settled, vast area that needed to be linked together by roads and canals for trade, travel, defense, and communications. The newly formed state governments in this area did not have either the population or the tax base to undertake ambitious projects. Thus, the populace turned to the federal government for assistance.[7] They also began to support a new political party that appeared after the War of 1812, the Whig party, which included in its platform the support of federally sponsored internal improvement projects.[8]

In the endeavor to obtain federal assistance for internal improvement projects, westerners were partially successful. Curtis Nettels calculated that forty federal appropriations, totalling slightly more than $1 million and 4 million acres of land, were made between 1815 and 1829, based on "conditions peculiar to the West."[9] Nettels divided the grants into six categories: territorial roads, roads within states permitted by Indian treaties, roads across state lands owned by Indians, roads and canals crossing public lands, navigation improvements on the Ohio and Mississippi rivers, and the National Road.[10] All of these grants tended to weaken the case of the strict constitutional constructionists by their mere presence on the statute books.

In addition to the growth of the West in political power after
the War of 1812, which led to more demands for internal improvement projects sponsored by the federal government, the growing
feelings of nationalism during and after the war intensified the feelings of frustration and anger felt by many people in the United States
in the wake of the largely disastrous land battles fought by this
country in the war. These battles demonstrated that the West could
not be adequately defended, given the crude transportation systems
existing there.[11] A House committee on December 15, 1817, summed
up this point of view well:

> The embarrassments of the nation during [the] war, from the
> want of good roads and canals, both in relation to trade and the
> transportation of cannon and military stores, have been too recently
> and sensibly felt to be forgotten. Vested with the power of making
> war, the Constitution could never have intended the General Gov-
> ernment should make it under such disadvantages.[12]

This position was echoed by John C. Calhoun, a "War Hawk" during the War of 1812, in a speech he delivered to the House on
January 31, 1816.[13] Henry Clay, another "War Hawk" and a Whig
party leader, also spoke approvingly of internal improvements in a
House debate on the National Road on April 1 of this same year.[14]

Daniel Webster of Massachusetts, however, reflected much of
the uncertainty of many Federalists after the War of 1812. He
returned to the House in 1816 and felt a little uneasy in supporting
the nationalizing philosophy of Clay and Calhoun. However, many
Federalists could see a partisan advantage in supporting internal
improvements because of the disagreement on this issue among
Republican politicians. For example, Webster voted in favor of
Calhoun's Bonus Bill of 1817,[15] and he was joined in that vote by
Rufus King of New York, the last presidential candidate of the
Federalist party. King shared Webster's cautious attitude on internal
improvements: while favoring roads and canals, he was doubtful of
the wisdom of financing them extensively.[16]

After the War of 1812, the first principal struggle among these
leaders, parties, and sections focused on Calhoun's Bonus Bill. The
bill's roots went back to February 8, 1808, when Senator Peter B.
Porter of New York made a lengthy speech in the Senate favoring
the construction of roads and canals and presented a resolution call-

ing for the appointment of a committee to examine "the expediency of appropriating a part of the public lands to such improvements."[17] The committee reported a bill that stipulated that the federal government should subscribe for one half of the stock of any corporation which had been, or which would be, chartered to carry on the works described by Albert Gallatin in his elaborate *Report of the Secretary of the Treasury, on the Subject of Public Roads and Canals. . . ,* which was published on April 8, 1808.[18] There the matter rested until the close of the war.

In mid-December, 1816, a memorial from a New York commission was submitted to the House that requested federal aid for a canal. The memorial was supported by Calhoun, who moved on December 16 "that a committee be appointed to enquire into the expediency of setting apart the bonus, and the net annual proceeds, of the National Bank, as a permanent fund for internal improvement."[19] This resolution was referred to a House committee headed by Calhoun, who reported a bill on December 23, 1816, "to set apart and pledge as a permanent fund for internal improvements the bonus of the national bank and the United States' share of its dividends."[20]

House debate on Calhoun's Bonus Bill climaxed on February 4, 1817, with great speeches by both Calhoun and Clay. Calhoun led off in defense of his bill. He dwelt on the increase of wealth that roads and canals would bring, on the service they would render in war, and most importantly, on the strength of union that would result from them. He concluded: "Whatever . . . impedes the intercourse of the extremes with . . . the centre of the Republic, weakens the union. . . . Let us then . . . bind the Republic together with a perfect system of roads and canals. Let us conquer space."[21] Clay echoed Calhoun's remarks and also said that he was not worried about the constitutionality of the Bonus Bill because a fund could be accumulating while the constitutionality of the bill was being decided.[22]

On March 1, 1817, the heavily amended Bonus Bill was passed by Congress. The House vote had been close: 86 to 84; the Senate had passed the bill by a vote of 20 to 15.[23] An analysis of the vote is interesting because it shows the stands of parties and sections of the country on the internal improvements question. In both branches of Congress the support of New York and Pennsylvania was crucial in the passage of the bill. Later, as both states began to develop their own internal improvement systems, they voted against national measures.[24] In the House, 33 of the "nay" votes on the bill were cast by New England Federalists. From the South there were 42 votes against the measure, but the southern vote was badly split. However, only ". . . twenty-five or thirty members, in the total number of one hundred and seventy, regarded the Constitutional difficulty as fatal to the bill."[25] The Senate vote was confused, too. The old Republicans' bloc "seemed to command not more than five or six votes. . . ."[26] What opposition there was in the Senate was divided between Federalists in New England and Republicans in the South. Western senators, as did their House colleagues, voted solidly in favor of the Bonus Bill. In short, "the divisions on this bill seemed to leave no question that Congress by an overwhelming majority regarded the Constitutional point as settled."[27]

Calhoun was confident of victory for his Bonus Bill when he visited the soon-to-be-retired President James Madison, who, like his predecessor, Thomas Jefferson, was not a strict constructionist when it came to the issue of internal improvements. In his public statements he called for a constitutional amendment to give Congress the power to aid improvement projects. However, during his administration, Madison did sign bills allotting $568,800 for road improvements. Most of this amount went to the National Road project, but $6,800 went for roads in Ohio, $8,000 for roads in Illinois, and $14,000 for other public road outlays.[28] One can well imagine Calhoun's shock when the president told him that he would veto the Bonus Bill. Calhoun could not persuade Madison to change his mind.[29]

On March 3, 1817, as his final official act as president, Madison vetoed the Bonus Bill. The power proposed to be exercised, he wrote to Congress, was not among the powers enumerated in the Constitution. It could not be included in the power to regulate commerce without departing from the meaning of words. To base it on a power to spend for the common defense and general welfare, Madison asserted, would give Congress a sweeping power of legislation on all subjects, with money being the ordinary means of executing all important acts. Madison's constitutional position contained the seeds of its own undoing, however, because he admitted he would have signed the Bonus Bill except for "insufficient precedents." In the process he ignored all the measures that he and his predecessors had approved.[30] One of Madison's biographers has written, "Had Madison's repeated recommendations of a federal system of roads and canals been based on imperative economic necessity or the urgent requirements of humanity, the constitutional authority probably would have seemed . . . adequate to him. . . ."[31]

Madison's veto had only a momentary effect on New York's plan to build the Erie Canal and other canals. New York's legislature decided to go ahead with the projects. At the same time, the Pennsylvania legislature appropriated half a million dollars for roads and canals. Actually, the veto of the Bonus Bill proved to be most injurious to the internal improvement programs in the southern states.[32]

Jefferson wrote approvingly to George Ticknor about Madison's veto: "He recommended an application to the states for an extension of their powers to this object, which will I believe be unanimously conceded, & will be a better way of obtaining the end, than by strained constructions. . . ." Jefferson added, "In the mean time the states separately are going on with this work. New York is undertaking the most gigantic enterprise of uniting the waters of L. Erie and the Hudson; Jersey those of the Delaware & Raritan."[33]

The day after Madison's veto of the Bonus Bill, the new president, James Monroe, delivered his first inaugural address. In his March 4 address, Monroe spoke in favor of roads and canals built with federal assistance, but only after Congress had been given the power by a constitutional amendment. Once the internal improvements had been completed, the new president said, "we shall add much to the convenience and comfort of our fellow-citizens, much to the ornament of the country, and . . . we shall bind the Union more closely together."[34]

The effect of Madison's Bonus Bill veto on the new president is made clear in a November 24, 1817, letter that Monroe wrote to Madison:

> The question respecting canals & roads is full of difficulty, growing out of what has passed on it. After all the consideration I have given it, I am fixed in the opinion, that the right is not in Congress and that it would be improper in me, after your negative, to allow them to discuss the subject & bring a bill for me to sign, in the expectation that I would do it.[35]

Madison wrote back to his successor and said, "The course you mean to take in relation to Roads & Canals, appears to be best adapted to the posture in which you find the case."[36]

Monroe was true to his word. In his first annual message to Congress, December 2, 1817, Monroe reiterated his view that the authority for internal improvements was lacking and that a constitutional amendment was the way out of the difficulty.[37]

The committee appointed by Congress to look into this part of Monroe's message did not agree with the chief executive. The committee reported that the actions of Monroe's predecessors had convinced them that the federal government could construct roads and canals without the sanction of a constitutional amendment. Specifically, the committee listed the following types of internal improvements that Congress had the power to construct: post roads through the states, with the assent of the latter; military roads, under the same conditions; canals for the purpose of interstate commerce; and canals for military purposes. It was the decision of the committee that Congress could appropriate funds but could not apply for projects. The report ended with the resolution "that the dividends from the stock in the National bank be set aside for internal improvements."[38] That was precisely what Calhoun had attempted to do with his Bonus Bill.

On March 6, 1818, the House went into a committee of the whole to debate the committee report. Verbal sparks flew for several days. On March 13, Clay came down from the Speaker's chair to deliver another great speech. He spoke for many Westerners when he described the need they felt for roads and canals and contrasted the federal government's attitude toward the interior regions with the government's eagerness to aid the eastern capitalists. He said he respected the rights of states, disavowing "that spirit of encroachment which would snatch from the States powers not delegated to the General Government." But when justice, patriotism, and economic need could be met by a liberal interpretation of the Constitution, he was for that construction:

> Every man who looks at the Constitution in the spirit to entitle him to the character of an American statesman, must elevate his views to the height which this nation is destined to reach in the rank of nations. We are not legislating for this moment only . . . but our acts must embrace a wider scope. . . .

Unfortunately, however, Clay turned from these lofty sentiments to a personal attack against the president. He condemned Monroe's December 2, 1817, message as being devoid of a single justification and implied that those who defended the president were sycophants and parasites.[39]

Following Clay's long speech, the House committee of the whole voted that Congress had the power to construct roads and canals. The vote, 89 to 75, was less than the two-thirds vote needed to pass over a certain presidential veto. Realizing this, several resolutions relating to congressional power to construct internal improvements were defeated, some measures by wide margins. The sense of the House having been determined, further consideration of the report was tabled.[40] The president had won, and Clay and his fellow supporters of federally sponsored internal improvement projects had suffered a humiliating defeat.

Undeterred, the House on March 30, 1818, requested Secretary of War Calhoun and Secretary of the Treasury William H. Crawford of Georgia, to report on military and civilian public works in progress and plans for aiding these.[41] The day after this House request, Calhoun wrote a revealing letter that showed the relationship of the South Carolinian with his superior: "You ask how the President and myself get along on constitutional questions. . . . The internal impr[ovemen]t question had been decided before my arrival at Washington. My sentiments are so well known in relation to the constitution, that he must expect . . . I will act in conformity with my established opinion."[42]

Therefore, Monroe could not have been surprised when his Secretary of War sent an elaborate report to the House on January 14, 1819. Calhoun ignored constitutional questions entirely and asserted that "a judicious system of roads and canals . . . by consolidating the Union, increasing its wealth and fiscal capacity, adds greatly to the resources of war."[43] As late as June, 1824, Calhoun was concocting grand programs for interlacing the country with roads and canals.[44]

The House tabled both Calhoun's ambitious program and the modest report Crawford had submitted on the financing of the projects because the Panic of 1819 depleted the federal treasury. Not until January 2, 1822, did the Committee on Roads and Canals in the House submit a bill, which recommended the following projects: a huge line of canals from the harbor of Boston south along the Atlantic Coast; a road from Washington, D.C., to New Orleans; a canal around the falls of the Ohio River at Louisville; a canal between the Ohio River and Lake Erie; a canal between the Susquehanna River and the Seneca and Genesee rivers, and another canal connecting the Tennessee River and the Savannah River.[45] The Committee on Roads and Canals had succeeded in incorporating the major features of both Gallatin's report of 1808 and Calhoun's 1819 report.[46] But this plan was relegated to the shelf along with its predecessors.[47]

Action in the internal improvements sphere shifted from reports and plans to the National (or Cumberland) Road. This great work had been constructed from Cumberland, Maryland, to Wheeling, Virginia, by 1818.[48] Following the end of the Panic of 1819 and stimulated by new state improvement projects, the Seventeenth Congress acted with energy. On December 12, 1821, a resolution was submitted to the Committee on Roads and Canals requesting them to examine the expediency of repairing the National Road and establishing toll gates on the road. Another resolution requested Monroe to report on the state of the National Road. Both resolutions were adopted by the House.[49]

The House passed a bill on April 29, 1822, appropriating nine thousand dollars for the repair of the National Road. To facilitate payment of future repair bills, the president was authorized to place toll gates along the road and to appoint toll gatherers. By fixing toll charges and penalties for nonpayment in the bill itself, it assumed the federal government had not only the power of appropriating and expending money for road construction, but also the power of operating the road and jurisdiction over it. The vote in the House is interesting. It was split along sectional lines, 87 to 68. An indifferent New England was evenly divided. New York, fearing competition for its own Erie Canal (then nearly completed), opposed it. Pennsylvania, which had also supported the Bonus Bill, now was divided because the state was in the middle of a massive program of internal improvement. Virginia, South Carolina, and Georgia lined up solidly against it. Maryland stood with the Old Northwest and Clay's Kentucky for the measure. The Senate passed the bill by a count of 29 to 7.[50]

On May 4, 1822, Monroe returned the National Road bill with his objections. He said the bill implied a power to build a complete system of internal improvements by the federal government, with the right of jurisdiction and sovereignty. He wrote, "I am of [the] opinion that Congress do not possess this power; that the States individually can not grant it, . . ."[51]

Accompanying this brief veto was Monroe's longest state paper: *Views of the President of the United States on the Subject of Internal Improvements*. This elaborate fifty-one-page report had been in the works since 1819, but then he had been dissuaded by John Quincy Adams, Calhoun, and Crawford from submitting it to Congress. This time, Monroe did not reveal his plans to his cabinet, knowing what their reaction would be.[52] In *Views*, the president went over the constitutional history of internal improvements and repeated his philosophy of the construction of the Constitution, and discussed the relation of the states and the federal government under the theory of divided sovereignty or dual federalism, similar to the view of James Madison. Somewhat confusedly, Monroe denied to the federal government the right of jurisdiction and sovereignty at the same time he asserted that Congress had unlimited power to raise money and that "in its appropriation, they have a discretionary power, restricted only by their duty to appropriate it to purposes of common defense and of general, not local, national, not state, benefit." In spite of this cautious attitude, Monroe did strongly recommend a system of internal improvements, if a constitutional amendment would authorize them.[53] Both houses of Congress went along with the president's veto.[54]

Congress did move ahead on several fronts: a rivers and harbors bill was passed and was signed by the president on March 3, 1823.[55] Furthermore, the Congress committed itself to a policy of patronizing canal projects when $300,000 was subscribed to the stock of the Chesapeake and Delaware Canal Company.[56] A number of roads were also opened or continued by the Congress, but the appropriations for these were paltry, ranging from $3,000 to $30,000 for each.[57] Nearly $498,000 was appropriated for the National Road; but the major portion of this total ($313,000) was merely to pay demands against former contracts, and only a small portion, $150,000, was actually applied to repair and extend the road, from Canton to Zanesville, Ohio.[58]

More important than any of these measures was the General Survey Bill of April 30, 1824. In the debate on the bill, Clay made a concerted effort to commit Congress to exercising the power to construct interstate highways and canals. He refreshed his colleagues' memories by recalling that Congress had approved laws for the construction of public buildings and lighthouses, coast surveys, and erection of sea walls in the Atlantic Coast states. In short, he said, "every thing, on the margin of the ocean. But nothing for domestic trade; nothing for the great interior of the country!" He also asserted that the right to regulate commerce granted Congress the power to construct roads and canals for the benefit of circulation and trade in the interior as it did the power to promote coastal trade. At another point in the debate, he exclaimed, "A new world has come into being since the Constitution was adopted. Are the narrow limited necessities of the old thirteen States, . . . as they existed at the formation of the present Constitution, forever to remain a rule of its interpretation?"[59]

The southern opposition to Clay's western vision was summarized by the brilliant and erratic John Randolph of Roanoke, Virginia. He painted a black picture of the results of the General Survey Bill, stating that if Congress possessed the power to do what the bill proposed, they might also have the power to free every slave in the Union, "and with stronger color of reason than they can exercise the power now contended for." Randolph closed his diatribe by threatening to form associations to oppose the bill and "every other means short of actual insurrection." He also made the following promise: "We shall keep on the windward side of treason."[60] However, Randolph's January 30, 1824, speech did raise the ugly spectre of disunion and civil war.

The final vote on the General Survey Bill in the House is revealing: New England gave 12 votes in favor and 26 votes against; the middle states gave 37 "yea" and 26 "nay"—New York supplying the bulk of the "nay" votes; the South registered 23 votes in favor and 34 votes against; and the West cast a unanimous 43 votes for the bill. The bill carried by 115 to 86.[61]

The General Survey Bill provided for surveys, plans, and estimates of the routes of such roads and canals as the president should deem of national importance. Monroe signed the bill the same day it cleared the Congress. As a first installment, thirty thousand dollars were appropriated, but a large number of appropriations were authorized later to carry out the provisions of the act.[62]

Although Monroe signed this bill, there was general frustration in many parts of the country with the Monroe administration's failure to adopt a comprehensive program of internal improvement along the lines outlined in Gallatin's and Calhoun's ambitious plans.[63] The Erie Canal, which was almost completed by 1824, provided a model for state-directed internal improvement projects. New York raised the necessary $8 million for the project by land sales, taxes on salt and auctions, lotteries, appropriations from the state legislature, and tolls.[64] Although the states of the Old Northwest did not have New York's economic advantages, they went ahead with several ambitious projects that ultimately failed. These projects are discussed in other papers in this volume. The federal government's role in assisting the states to complete these projects was limited to the donation of public lands for revenues: "Up to 1830, a total of 2,586 square miles of public lands was given by Congress to aid the canal projects of Ohio, Indiana, and Illinois."[65]

Monroe's ambivalence concerning internal improvements is readily seen in two stands he took on National Road legislation: in 1822 he vetoed a bill concerning it, and in 1825 he signed a bill that provided for its extension. Monroe's wayward course might seem to be a natural indecisiveness or a reflection of his political attitudes. One of his biographers contends that Monroe saw the importance of internal improvements, supported some limited measures in the interim to bring them about, but eventually wanted a constitutional amendment "to confine federal legislation to great national works, leaving all minor improvements to the separate states."[66]

Whatever the cause of Monroe's caution concerning internal improvements, it did not endear him to the people of the interior. There was a good deal of bad feeling in the West during the Era of Good Feelings. The following appeared in an Ohio newspaper in 1823: "There is a party of politicians at Washington, whose consciences are so tender, or whose minds are so contracted, that no general system of internal improvements can be anticipated, from the councils of the nation, until there is a radical change in the Executive departments."[67]

In the 1824 presidential election, western leaders saw a chance to make this "radical change" by backing Henry Clay for president and by embracing Clay's "American System." By 1824, Clay had pulled together the essential elements of his system, but they were "never joined together into a nicely articulated whole."[68] The important elements of the system were a protective tariff to aid American industries, internal improvements at national expense, the use of the public lands for these improvements, and the maintenance of the Bank of the United States to insure a stable currency.[69] Clay's program was not greeted with universal applause. In a March 29, 1830, speech in Congress, James K. Polk characterized the "American System" as "a tripod . . . a stool that stands upon three legs. . . . The third branch of the system is internal improvements, which is the sponge which is to suck up the excess of revenue."[70]

This hostile reaction toward Clay's program is a sample of the wide splits that quickly developed because "Clay's matured political philosophy was an amalgam of Jeffersonian and Federalist principles."[71] By the end of Monroe's one-party presidency, therefore, political thought became polarized. If not solely responsible for the rise of a two-party spirit, Clay's system did nothing to hinder this development. The "American System" attracted eastern manufacturers, speculators, and western men who envisioned the development of their section. Opponents of the system included southern planters and many farmers from all sections, who saw tariffs as raising prices and internal improvements as increasing taxes.[72] Frederick Jackson Turner has stated that the controversy over the "American System" divided the nation in a sectional way, too,[73] but each section favored certain portions of the system and rejected other portions, largely on the grounds of economic self-interest.

As to Clay's motives in creating the "American System," historians have never reached agreement. While not denying Clay's economic interest in tariffs and improvements because he had money tied up in Kentucky hemp, Clement Eaton has stated that Clay's ideas were part of a broad nationalism, each section of the system "beautifully integrated" to assist in the development of the United States.[74] On the other hand, George Dangerfield is more skeptical of Clay's political and economic motives: "Might it not be said that, if Mr. Clay dreamed the great American dream, he did so with one eye open, and that the open eye was in rapt contemplation of the interests of Eastern monopoly?"[75] William A. Williams agrees with Dangerfield's view, but he also praises Clay for his realism: "He tried very hard to adjust the ideology of laissez faire to the realities of America through a reinvigoration of his mercantilist American System, and then to institutionalize that resolution in a political party."[76] Initially, that party was the National Republican, a short-lived group that was led by John Quincy Adams following his controversial victory (with the assistance of Clay in the House) in the 1824 presidential election.

The thoughts of the new president with regard to internal improvements were as straightforward and progressive as his predecessor's had been cautious and conservative: "The first *duty* of a nation . . . [is] that of bettering its own condition by internal improvement."[77] Indeed, internal improvements formed a central part of Adams's political philosophy. As one historian has noted: "Adams . . . asserted that it was man's duty to act through government for the improvement of his condition. Only thus might the rights of all be realized through the efforts of all."[78] This expansive view embraced city planning, aid to business, scientific research, as well as road and canal construction.[79] Adams's views were so advanced that he succeeded in isolating himself from many allies. As Secretary of State in the Monroe cabinet, he had tried to convince Monroe that internal improvements were necessary to national development, but only Calhoun supported his views.[80] He alienated himself from members of his old party, the Federalist, by his espousal of federally sponsored internal improvement projects.[81] He spoke forthrightly concerning the need for national direction in the internal improvements area in his inaugural address of March 4, 1825,[82] and in his first annual message to Congress on December 6, 1825,[83] but both speeches stirred up much criticism.[84]

Despite the uproar generated by Adams's 1825 messages, a large number of projects were started during his administration. For the first time, land was granted for the promotion of various projects involving roads, canals, and river improvements. Specific canal projects in the Old Northwest are discussed in other papers in this volume. Other projects included a road from Columbus to Sandusky in Ohio[85] and river improvements in Alabama.[86] During 1825, almost $644,000 was spent on the National Road, and the federal government, in a carry-over from the final days of the Monroe administration, bought stock in the following canal companies: Louisville and Portland, Dismal Swamp, Chesapeake and Ohio, and Chesapeake and Delaware.[87] Over $2.3 million was appropriated for internal improvements by the Adams administration, compared with $1 million appropriated during all the previous administrations.[88]

It should be noted that many projects undertaken during the Adams presidency were not part of any great national program. Adams was not able to control federal legislation on the subject, and states and private corporations were far ahead of the national government in these undertakings. Congress decided to follow Monroe's philosophy, not Adams's, by making appropriations for improvements, while at the same time refusing to construct these projects or exercise federal jurisdiction over them.[89] To one scholar, this change from federal to state and corporate control of most improvement enterprises had advantages because federal-state co-operation was enhanced in succeeding decades.[90] James Madison in an 1826 letter to Martin Van Buren attempted to give one cause for the shift from federal to state improvement programs during the Adams administration: in the absence of a constitutional amendment spelling out the precise relationships between state and federal gov-ernment in this area, the drift to state improvement programs would continue unless such an amendment were eventually passed.[91]

Sometime during the first part of Adams's administration, Vice-President Calhoun turned his back on internal improvements, a cause he had long championed. In this political shift, Calhoun reflected changes that were occurring in the South. In 1826 he moved back to his native South Carolina and took the pulse of his former constitu-ents. He found no great love for internal improvements among them, and his rising political ambitions got the better of his former nationalistic principles. Thus, the man whom Daniel J. Elazar calls the "greatest single architect" of American federalism became an ardent states'-rights man.[92]

With Calhoun's renunciation of the "American System" and Secretary of State Clay's preoccupation with foreign affairs, the main burden of supporting internal improvements fell on Daniel Webster. In an 1828 speech in Boston, Webster, after reviewing the history of internal improvements, said, "I am among those who have held the opinion, that, if any object of that kind be of general and national importance, it is within the scope of the powers of the government; though I admit it to be a power which should be exer-cised with very great care and discretion." He went on to say that public improvements in all sections of the country had to be under-taken in order to "render the Constitution perpetual. . . ."[93]

One month after Webster's Boston speech, two symbolic acts

took place that illustrate the rapid change in transportation modes during the Transportation Revolution. In Washington, D.C., on July 4, 1828, President Adams turned the first shovel of earth to signal the beginning of the Chesapeake and Ohio Canal. But on the same day in Baltimore, the last surviving signer of the Declaration of Independence, Charles Carroll of Carrollton, performed a historically more important act in laying a foundation stone to signify the start of construction of the Baltimore and Ohio Railroad. In the end, the railroad replaced the canal.[94]

Adams was not only out of step in terms of the Transportation Revolution, but also in terms of political realities. He dreamed of a return to the nonpartisan politics of the Monroe era. He kept many pro-Andrew Jackson supporters in office and in his own cabinet, where they effectively sabotaged anything he might do. Calhoun, Adams's own vice-president, worked actively against him. It seemed inevitable that the "Hero of New Orleans," Andrew Jackson, would sweep Adams out of office in the 1828 presidential election, and the subsequent Jackson landslide did not surprise the prognosticators.[95]

Jackson's record on internal improvements before the 1828 election was so confused that few people could predict how he would approach the problem during his administration. In 1822, Jackson wrote President Monroe in support of the latter's veto of a National Road bill.[96] Jackson was briefly in the Senate in 1823–1824 and voted consistently for internal improvements, including the Survey Bill of 1824 and the river improvement bill of the same year. Both measures were signed by President Monroe; thus Jackson was not going against his old friend in his voting.[97] However, he did state in an 1824 letter that the federal government could not begin a project without a state's consent. Significantly, in the light of Jackson's subsequent action as president, he added, "Jealousy and the fear of encroachment by the general govt. ought not to form a pretext for denying to her the exercise of those powers which may be derived from a liberal construction of the Constitution."[98]

Inconsistent presidential candidates appeared long before the mid-twentieth century. In the 1828 presidential campaign, Jackson men in the West asserted that "Old Hickory" was a friend of internal improvements and the "American System." The Clay vote was being wooed there. In the East, and especially in Martin Van Buren's New York, a different Jackson was on display. There, Jackson was quoted as being in favor of state projects, such as the Erie Canal.[99] Jackson seemed a little annoyed at the attempts to make him seem to be all things to all men. Earlier, he had written to an army officer, "In my public acts, as well as private, I have always viewed honesty the best policy and pursued it."[100] But the general's political managers apparently disagreed with such openness, and the favorable results of the 1828 election would seem to vindicate their tactics.

The draft of Jackson's first inaugural address, March 4, 1829, gave more clues to the course he would take than his official address. In the draft, the president stated that the surplus revenues from the tariff could be distributed among the states, according to their representation, for use in education and internal improvements.[101] This idea was made public in Jackson's first annual message to Congress, December 8, 1829. While conceding that "every member of the Union, in peace and in war, will be benefited by the improvement of inland navigation and the construction of highways in the several States," he pointed out that the use of the previous method had generated controversy on the grounds of constitutionality and expediency. Along with recommending the apportionment of federal surplus revenue among the states for use in internal improvements, Jackson also stated that "should this measure not be found warranted by the Constitution . . . it would be expedient to propose to the States an amendment authorizing it."[102]

In a letter written soon after his first annual message, Jackson expressed the hope that his plan would end *"logg-rolling legislation. . . ."* He closed the letter with an adverse comment on his vice-president, Calhoun: "I feel the more anxious about this [my plan], because I have reason to believe a decided stand will be taken by the friends of Mr. Calhoun, in Congress, against the policy, if not the constitutionality, of such a measure."[103]

However, it was Daniel Webster, not Jackson, who led the counterattack against Calhoun's stand on internal improvements. On January 18, 1830, Webster introduced a petition from the South Carolina Canal and Railroad Company that requested the federal government to subscribe to its capital stock.[104] Calhoun joined South Carolina Senators Robert Y. Hayne and William Smith in refusing to support the petition because he felt it violated the principle of states' rights.[105]

Webster enlarged on his support of internal improvements in a great speech he delivered in the Senate on January 26, 1830. Ostensibly it was a reply to Senator Hayne, but it was actually an attack on Calhoun, who was presiding in the Senate. Webster attempted to refute the South Carolina charge that New England in general and Daniel Webster in particular were only recent supporters of internal improvements and that they were using this issue as a form of intimidation directed against the South. Webster stated that he had supported improvement projects at national expense since 1816, and New England had supported these projects before the War of 1812. He contended that he did not want an unjustified expansion of the powers of the federal government, but he felt that internal improvements could be undertaken under the powers stipulated in the Constitution.

Turning from this line of attack, Webster accused "leading gentlemen" from South Carolina of recently changing their opinions with respect to internal improvements. Everyone in the audience knew of whom he spoke. Then he said, "up to 1824, I . . . followed South Carolina; but when that star, in its ascension, veered off in an unexpected direction, I relied on its light no longer." Calhoun could contain himself no longer and blurted out, "Does the chair understand the gentleman . . . to say that the person now occupying the chair of the Senate has changed his opinions on the subject of internal improvements?" Webster replied, "If such change has taken place, I regret it."[106]

Shortly after Webster's speech condemning Calhoun's rejection of federally sponsored internal improvements, President Jackson launched the opening round in his attack on his political rival Henry Clay and his "American System." Internal improvements were the first target, specifically the Maysville Road.

This road, some sixty-four miles long, lay wholly within Kentucky. As was the case with most interior roads, it was in deplorable shape. Clay told a Cincinnati audience in August, 1830, that he and his family spent four days during the previous year in traveling its length.[107]

To assist in the improvement of the Maysville Road, the Kentucky legislature incorporated the Maysville, Washington, Paris, and Lexington Turnpike Road Company, which was to build a section of road along the Maysville path that connected the National Road at Zanesville, Ohio, to Florence, Alabama, on the Tennessee

River. This route had been surveyed by the U.S. Army engineers in
1827. Clearly, with connectors, the Maysville Road was interstate
in character. It was an important interstate link, too: during one
month a daily average of 31 carriages, 51 wagons, and 331 people
passed over it.[108]

A bill was introduced in the House on April 26, 1830, that provided for the federal government to subscribe $150,000 for stock in
the Maysville Turnpike Road Company.[109] There was nothing un-
usual about this subscription; since 1825 the federal government had
purchased a considerable amount of stock in internal improvement
corporations.

After an acrimonious debate in the House, the bill was passed on
April 29 by a vote of 102 to 96.[110] The Senate approved the measure
on May 15, with the upper chamber split on the same party lines
that existed in the House. Basically, the congressmen from the southeastern states joined with some colleagues from New York, New
England, and Tennessee in opposition to the bill.[111]

Martin Van Buren, even before the bill cleared the Senate, saw
an opportunity to strike a blow at Clay. He later recalled: "The road
was in Mr. Clay's own State and Mr. Clay was, the General thought
... pressing the measure and the question it involved upon him rather
for political effect than for public ends. . . ." In short, internal improvements were to become a political football. Van Buren brought
the bill to the attention of Jackson and also put his written thoughts
in the president's hands. Some of these thoughts appeared in the
completed veto message.[112] At least in his actions Van Buren remained consistent in his response to federally sponsored or assisted
internal improvement projects. As a New Yorker, he felt that other
states could very easily follow the example of New York and construct internal improvements without the assistance of the federal
government.[113]

On May 27, 1830, Jackson sent his veto of the Maysville Road
bill to Congress. The veto was greeted by considerable dismay on
the part of the president's western supporters.[114] Jackson tended to
base his veto on constitutional grounds, but his main contention was
that the road was local even within Kentucky and that by no stretch
of the imagination could the road be considered national in character: "It has no connection with any established system of improvements; is exclusively within the limits of a State. . . ." Jackson

contended that the lack of an adequate treasury surplus would stop even appropriations for works of a national character. He said he favored reducing federal taxation and paying off the national debt before undertaking more enterprises. He concluded his message by making the standard plea for a constitutional amendment to sanction federally sponsored improvement projects.[115]

The Maysville Road bill veto and the veto of the Washington Turnpike Road Company bill on May 31, 1830, on similar grounds[116] were clear-cut political acts, but historians have disagreed on the target, if any, for the vetoes. William A. Williams agrees with Van Buren and finds Clay to have been the main victim.[117] Gerald Capers insists that Calhoun was the principal target for Jackson.[118] Daniel J. Elazar reluctantly agrees that politics might have motivated the president's vetoes: "Jackson's apparently negative stand on the internal improvement issue is closely connected with the struggle for power within his administration family between [Secretary of State] Van Buren and [Vice-President] Calhoun."[119] Glyndon Van Deusen observes, "The veto was largely political, for Jackson signed some internal improvement bills fully as local as the Maysville Road. It was a slap at Clay, who had energetically pushed the Maysville Road, and at the American system."[120] Surprisingly, George Rogers Taylor does not mention the political causes and consequences of the veto. Instead, he indicates that Jackson opposed the bill because he saw it as a purely local project that was not part of a larger national system and possibly also because he opposed federal aid to a private corporation.[121]

Clay was stunned by the Maysville Road veto, but he quickly recovered and started to marshal anti-Jackson forces. He felt he had a ready-made issue for the 1832 presidential campaign. These ideas were expressed in a letter he wrote to Webster soon after the veto. "We shall attack the veto," he wrote, "by proposing an amendment of the constitution to restrict it, so as to require a majority of all the members elected to each branch of the Congress, instead of two thirds, subsequently, to pass the bill. . . ." Clay added this confident statement: "You can imagine, . . . what effect must be produced by this event. We were safe before. Now, I think, we may be considered as absolutely certain. . . ."[122]

Jackson and his lieutenants had correctly anticipated that the Maysville Road veto and other policy decisions would draw Clay out of retirement and into the presidential race. In discussing the Kentucky meetings that were being organized to protest Jackson's vetoes, Clay saw another purpose in the meetings: "It is thought by my friends that these public meetings will furnish suitable occasions for making a nomination for the next Presidency. . . ."[123]

The president, too, continued to issue confident statements to his friends throughout June and July, 1830: "The veto, has become what my enemies neither wished, or expected, very popular, I have no doubt but it will be sustained by a large majority of the people. . . ."[124] As events developed, it became clear that Jackson, not Clay, had correctly understood the mood of the majority of the American voters. For example, in the New York state elections of 1830, the Jackson men based their platform on the Maysville Road veto and "the just right of the States"—and won.[125]

Indeed, the New York vote substantiated what Jackson friends such as Felix Grundy and Martin Van Buren had been saying: the veto of primarily a local project would upset only the people in that location, in this case, Kentucky. Residents of the middle states, who were supporting state projects, would not applaud federal support of projects in less-fortunate states. In the South, planters who were blessed by adequate river transportation would also praise the veto.[126] In short, the Maysville Road veto was a master political stroke.

Clay decided not to attack the president directly in public. Therefore, his public pronouncements were directed at Van Buren and other members of the Jackson cabinet. In one speech in August, 1830, he characterized Van Buren as an American Talleyrand—a sly, unprincipled politician.[127] The Kentuckian received an unexpected ally when Madison protested to Van Buren that his veto of the Bonus Bill in 1817 had been misconstrued by President Jackson: "It was an object of the veto to deny to Congress as well the appropriating power, as the executing and jurisdictional branches of it."[128] Van Buren did his best to sooth the feelings of the former president, perhaps in an attempt to keep Clay and his followers from finding out about the discrepancies in the vetoes of the two presidents and using it for political advantage.[129]

Jackson was not as cautious as his chief adviser, Van Buren. Adding insult to Clay's injury, "Old Hickory" revealed in his second annual message to Congress, December 6, 1830, that he had pocket vetoed bills authorizing a subscription to the stock of the Louisville and Portland Canal Company and appropriating money for rivers, harbors, and lighthouses. In his message the president declared that bills relating to private corporations were improper because powers of the federal, state, and local governments should be kept distinct. If such subscriptions were made, he said, the power of the United States in local affairs will become "almost inconceivable," and "dangerous to the liberties of the people." The rivers and harbors bill was attacked because of the local nature of many of the projects in Jackson's opinion. Also, the president insisted that the total cost of the package would be $96 million; he considered that too extravagant. In a thinly veiled challenge to Clay, Jackson observed that if the American people were upset with his course, they would rise up in the 1832 presidential election and cast him out.[130] Apparently Jackson was not expecting this to happen.

Years after the Maysville veto, Thomas Hart Benton wrote in his reminiscences that that veto was "a killing blow" to the overall system of internal improvements.[131] Glyndon Van Deusen calls it "the beginning of the end for the long struggle over nationally constructed roads and canals."[132] By 1833, all of Clay's major proposals embodied in the "American System" had been ruined by the policies of Jackson and his followers,[133] and that same year a discouraged Clay wrote a friend and reflected on that fact:

> As to politics, we have no past, no future. After forty-four years of existence under the present Constitution, what single principle is fixed? The Bank? No. Internal Improvements? No. The Tariff? No. Who is to interpret the Constitution? We are as much afloat at sea as the day when the Constitution went into operation. There is nothing certain but that the will of Andrew Jackson is to govern; and that will fluctuates with the change of every pen which gives expression to it.[134]

Despite Clay's pessimism, internal improvements continued to be aided by the federal government during the Jackson presidency. In fact, almost five times as much money ($10,582,882) was spent on these projects during the Jackson administration than was spent during the Adams presidency.[135] The reason this happened was that while bills of an exclusively internal improvement nature died off in the face of a certain presidential veto they were often worked into a general appropriations bill. Then the president was faced with killing a major bill just to get rid of a few "pork barrel" measures.[136] Indeed, this method is still used by Congress to get presidential approval of controversial projects.

E. C. Nelson points out that internal improvement projects increased during the remaining years of the Jackson administration, but the signs of rot after 1830 were unmistakable. By 1834, the National Road was turned over to the states[137] and was extended into Illinois in a haphazard fashion. Purchases of private improvement corporation stock dropped off dramatically. Before the Civil War, only lighthouses and rivers and harbors improvement projects remained to remind people of once magnificent programs.

In defense of Jackson and his policies E. C. Nelson has written that most roads sponsored by the federal government were poorly constructed—a result, no doubt, of the graft, log-rolling, and general corruption that attended many of these projects. Stock in many of the improvement corporations proved to be bad investments because of poor management and undercapitalization. Railroads rapidly replaced most canals, which generally showed the effects of poor engineering from the beginning.[138]

But the consequences of state control and financing of internal improvement projects were equally disastrous, especially in the wake of the Panic of 1837. Some states had to repudiate improvement debts until the crisis was over. All six states in the Old Northwest changed their constitutions to outlaw state participation in improvement enterprises. Other states followed suit in a variety of other ways.[139] We may ask whether the absence of overall federal control or direction over internal improvement projects in the United States prior to 1837 may not have contributed to the chaos that followed.[140]

Within the context of the internal improvement issue during the 1816–1830 period, we can readily see which political leaders were more responsive to the needs of the country for internal development. On the national level at least, Clay, Adams, Gallatin, Webster, and Calhoun (down to 1824) showed more foresight in anticipating the future needs of the country by supporting national measures of improvement. These men were also more inclined to approve federal-state co-operation (as opposed to the dual federalism concept of James Madison) and government ownership of the stock of private internal improvement corporations. On the other hand, Jefferson, Madison, Monroe, Jackson, Van Buren, and Calhoun (after 1824) were alarmed by the loose construction of the Constitution that seemed to accompany the sanction of federally sponsored internal improvement projects. Initially, these men harkened back to a simpler agrarian past and favored laissez-faire economics over the mercantilist ideas espoused by the first group of leaders. Glyndon Van Deusen has concluded that "the Whig attitude toward the function of government, at least on the national level, bears a closer resemblance to that of the New Deal than did the attitude toward government of Jackson and Van Buren."[141]

Also, increasingly after the War of 1812, the strict adherence to constitutional principles began to give way to sectional and economic pressures that brought about much political change. In the halls of Congress and in the White House, self-interest began to dominate in place of high-minded constitutional principles. Some historians have called this sectional self-interest the "animating influences" in the breakdown of national control over internal development.[142] Without national direction, the United States suffered through many costly failures of misguided private and state development projects.

The Maysville Road veto of 1830 was a decisive turning point in the history of internal development in this country; it would take almost a century for national development to recover from the effects of it and sectional fragmentation. Jackson, as other presidents after him, used the issue of national development to work his political will, under the gloss of confused "principles." In the end, national development was sacrificed on the altar of political expediency.

NOTES

1. Charles L. Dearing, *American Highway Policy* (Washington, D.C.: The Brookings Institution, 1941), p. 58.

2. Frederick Jackson Turner, *Rise of the New West, 1819–1829* (New York: Harper & Bros., 1907), p. 6.

3. Curtis Nettels, "The Mississippi Valley and the Constitution, 1815–29," in *Mississippi Valley Historical Review*, XI (1924–1925), 332.

4. *Ibid.*, pp. 348–49.

5. *Ibid.*, p. 332.

6. *Ibid.*, p. 354.

7. *Ibid.*, pp. 333–34.

8. Logan Esarey, *Internal Improvements in Early Indiana* (Indiana Historical Society *Publications*, V, Indianapolis, 1912), p. 78.

9. Nettels, "The Mississippi Valley and the Constitution, 1815–29," in *Mississippi Valley Historical Review*, XI, 342.

10. *Ibid.*

11. Esarey, *Internal Improvements in Indiana*, p. 48.

12. *Annals of Congress*, 15 Cong., 1 Sess., 457.

13. Robert L. Meriwether and W. Edwin Hemphill (eds.), *The Papers of John C. Calhoun* (13 volumes to date. Columbia: University of South Carolina Press, 1959–), I, 326.

14. James F. Hopkins and Margaret W. M. Hargreaves (eds.), *The Papers of Henry Clay* (6 volumes to date. Lexington: University of Kentucky Press, 1959–), II, 187–88.

15. Richard N. Current, *Daniel Webster and the Rise of National Conservatism* (Boston: Little, Brown & Co., 1955), p. 19.

16. King to Christopher Gore, November 5, 1816, in Charles R. King (ed.), *The Life and Correspondence of Rufus King . . .* (6 volumes. New York: G. P. Putnam's Sons, 1894–1900), VI, 34; King to Thomas Worthington, February 21 and March 1, 1817, in *ibid.*, pp. 60, 65n; *Annals of Congress*, 13 Cong., 3 Sess., 188–89.

17. *Annals of Congress*, 11 Cong., 2 Sess., 1385ff.

18. *Ibid.*, 13 Cong., 2 Sess., 1935–41. For Gallatin's report see *American State Papers: Miscellaneous* (1834), I, 724–41.

19. Meriwether and Hemphill (eds.), *Calhoun Papers*, I, 368.

20. *Ibid.*, p. 372.

21. *Ibid.*, pp. 398–407. The quotation is on page 401.

22. Hopkins and Hargreaves (eds.), *Clay Papers*, II, 308–11.

23. *Annals of Congress*, 14 Cong., 2 Sess., 109–12, 185–88, 934, and 1051–52.

24. George Rogers Taylor, *The Transportation Revolution, 1815–1860* (New York: Rinehart & Co., 1951), p. 21.

25. Henry Adams, *History of the United States during the Administrations of Jefferson and Madison* (9 volumes. New York: C. Scribner's Sons, 1890–1909), IX, 150.

26. *Ibid.*, p. 151.

27. *Ibid.*

28. E. C. Nelson, "Presidential Influence in the Policy of Internal Improvements," in *Iowa Journal of History and Politics*, IV (1906), Appendix A, p. 56.

29. Gerald M. Capers, *John C. Calhoun—Opportunist: A Reappraisal* (Gainesville: University of Florida Press, 1960), pp. 54–55.

30. James D. Richardson (comp.), *A Compilation of the Messages and Papers of the Presidents, 1789–1897* (Washington, D.C.: Government Printing Office, 1897), I, 584–85.

31. Irving Brant, *James Madison* (6 volumes. Indianapolis: Bobbs-Merrill Co., 1941–1961), VI, 417.

32. Adams, *History of the United States*, IX, 169.

33. Jefferson to Ticknor, May [?], 1817, in Paul L. Ford (ed.), *The Works of Thomas Jefferson* (12 volumes. New York: G. P. Putnam's Sons, 1904–1905), XII, 59. Also see Jefferson to Baron F. H. Alexander von Humboldt, June 13, 1817, in *ibid.*, p. 69, and Jefferson to Albert Gallatin, June 16, 1817, in *ibid.*, pp. 71–72.

34. Richardson (comp.), *Messages and Papers*, II, 8.

35. Monroe to Madison, November 24, 1817, in Stanislaus Hamilton (ed.), *The Writings of James Monroe* (7 volumes. New York: G. P. Putnam's Sons, 1898–1903), VI, 32.

36. Madison to Monroe, November 29, 1817, in Gaillard Hunt (ed.), *The Writings of James Madison* (9 volumes. New York: G. P. Putnam's Sons, 1900–1910), VIII, 397.

37. Richardson (comp.), *Messages and Papers*, II, 17–18.

38. *Annals of Congress*, 15 Cong., 1 Sess., 405, 451, 1114, 1138, and 1249.

39. *Ibid.*, 1359–80. Also printed in Hopkins and Hargreaves (eds.), *Clay Papers*, II, 461–91.

40. *Annals of Congress*, 15 Cong., 1 Sess., 1385–88.

41. *Ibid.*, 1649–79.

42. Calhoun to John G. Jackson, March 31, 1818, in Meriwether and Hemphill (eds.), *Calhoun Papers*, II, 216.

43. *American State Papers: Miscellaneous*, II, 533ff. Also see *Annals of Congress*, 15 Cong., 1 Sess., 2443.

44. Nathan Sargent, *Public Men and Events* ... (2 volumes. Philadelphia: J. B. Lippincott & Co., 1875), I, 26.

45. *Annals of Congress*, 17 Cong., 1 Sess., 606.

46. William P. Cresson, *James Monroe* (Chapel Hill: University of North Carolina Press, 1946), p. 390.

47. Nelson, "Presidential Influence in the Policy of Internal Improvements," in *Iowa Journal of History and Politics*, IV, 28.

48. Turner, *Rise of the New West*, p. 230. For background and an assessment of the National Road's importance see Esarey, *Internal Improvements in Indiana*, pp. 53–55, and Jeremiah S. Young, *A Political and Constitutional Study of the Cumberland Road* (Chicago: University of Chicago Press, 1904).

49. *Annals of Congress*, 17 Cong., 1 Sess., 560, 577.

50. *Ibid.*, 1734 and 1872; Cresson, *James Monroe*, p. 392; and Turner, *Rise of the New West*, p. 231.

51. Richardson (comp.), *Messages and Papers*, II, 142–43.

52. Nelson, "Presidential Influence in the Policy of Internal Improvements," in *Iowa Journal of History and Politics*, IV, 29.

53. Richardson (comp.), *Messages and Papers*, II, 144–83. For another printing see Hamilton (ed.), *Monroe Writings*, VI, 216–84. For an analysis of Monroe's views see Nettels, "Mississippi Valley and the Constitution, 1815–29," in *Mississippi Valley Historical Review*, XI, 347–48.

54. Turner, *Rise of the New West*, p. 232.

55. U.S. *Statutes at Large*, III, 761.

56. *Ibid.,* IV, 124.

57. Nelson, "Presidential Influence in the Policy of Internal Improvements," in *Iowa Journal of History and Politics,* IV, Appendix A, pp. 56–60.

58. U.S. *Statutes at Large,* III, 426, 604, 728; IV, 128.

59. *Annals of Congress,* 18 Cong., 1 Sess., 1035 and 1315.

60. *Ibid.,* 1296–1311. This speech is conveniently reprinted in Russell Kirk, *John Randolph of Roanoke: A Study in American Politics . . .* (Chicago: Regnery, 1964), pp. 337–57.

61. Turner, *Rise of the New West,* p. 235.

62. U.S. *Statutes at Large,* IV, 629, 703, 777, V, 69.

63. Cresson, *James Monroe,* pp. 396–97.

64. George Dangerfield, *The Era of Good Feelings* (New York: Harcourt, Brace & World, 1963), pp. 322–23. Also see Ronald E. Shaw, *Erie Water West: A History of the Erie Canal, 1792–1854* (Lexington: University of Kentucky Press, 1966) for a comprehensive history of the canal and its economic impact on New York and the nation.

65. Francis S. Philbrick, *The Rise of the West, 1754–1830* (New York: Harper & Row, 1966), p. 334.

66. Cresson, *James Monroe,* p. 395.

67. *National Republican and Ohio Political Register* (Cincinnati, Ohio), July 23, 1823, quoted in Homer C. Hockett, *Western Influences on Political Parties to 1825 . . .* (Columbus: Ohio State University, 1917), p. 132n.

68. Glyndon G. Van Deusen, *The Jacksonian Era, 1828–1848* (New York: Harper & Row, 1963), p. 51.

69. The main outlines of the "American System" can be found in Calvin Colton (ed.), *The Works of Henry Clay* (10 volumes. New York: G. P. Putnam's Sons, 1904), VI, 78–80, 108–10, 116–35, 218–37, 254–94; VII, 388–91, 395–400, 437–86, 524–35.

70. *Congressional Debates,* 21 Cong., 1 Sess., 698–99.

71. Clement Eaton, *Henry Clay and the Art of American Politics* (Boston: Little, Brown, 1957), p. 47. Also see Marvin Meyers, *The Jacksonian Persuasion: Politics and Belief* (Stanford, Calif.: Stanford University Press, 1957), pp. 13–15.

72. William N. Chambers, *Old Bullion Benton: Senator from the New West* (Boston: Little, Brown, 1956), pp. 119–20.

73. Frederick Jackson Turner, *The United States, 1830–1850: The Nation and Its Sections* (New York: Henry Holt & Co., 1935), p. 386.

74. Eaton, *Henry Clay,* pp. 45–46.

75. Dangerfield, *The Era of Good Feelings,* p. 120.

76. William A. Williams, *The Contours of American History* (Chicago: Quadrangle Books, 1966), p. 263.

77. Adams to James Lloyd, October 1, 1822, in Worthington C. Ford (ed.), *The Writings of John Quincy Adams* (7 volumes. New York: Macmillan Co., 1913–17), VII, 312.

78. George A. Lipsky, *John Quincy Adams: His Theory and Ideas* (New

York: Crowell, 1950), p. 146. Also see Adams to Benjamin Waterhouse, October 24, 1813, in Ford (ed.), *Writings of John Quincy Adams*, IV, 526–27.

79. Lipsky, *John Quincy Adams*, p. 146. Also see Adams's diary entry, January 13, 1831, in Charles F. Adams (ed.), *Memoirs of John Quincy Adams* (12 volumes. Philadelphia: J. B. Lippincott & Co., 1874–77), VIII, 273.

80. Lipsky, *John Quincy Adams*, pp. 147–48.

81. Shaw Livermore, Jr., *The Twilight of Federalism: The Disintegration of the Federalist Party, 1815–1830* (Princeton, N.J.: Princeton University Press, 1962), p. 217. For a contrary view see Adams to Clay, April 21, 1829, in Calvin Colton (ed.), *The Private Correspondence of Henry Clay* (New York: A. S. Barnes & Co., 1856), p. 227.

82. Richardson (comp.), *Messages and Papers*, II, 298–99.

83. *Ibid.*, p. 316.

84. George Dangerfield, *The Awakening of American Nationalism, 1815–1828* (New York: Harper & Row, 1965), p. 238.

85. U.S. *Statutes at Large*, IV, 242.

86. *Ibid.*, 290.

87. Nelson, "Presidential Influence in the Policy of Internal Improvements," in *Iowa Journal of History and Politics*, IV, Appendix A, pp. 58–59.

88. Henry G. Wheeler, *History of Congress . . .* (2 volumes. New York: Harper & Bros., 1848), II, 140, 190. Also see Turner, *Rise of the New West*, p. 288. For a discussion of the most extensive internal improvement program passed into law during the Adams presidency, that in 1828, see Nettels, "The Mississippi Valley and the Constitution, 1815–29," in *Mississippi Valley Historical Review*, XI, 352–53.

89. Turner, *Rise of the New West*, pp. 287–88, 293–94. Also see Adams's plea of February 21, 1828, for repair of the National Road in Richardson (comp.), *Messages and Papers*, II, 396.

90. Daniel J. Elazar, *The American Partnership: Intergovernmental Cooperation in the Nineteenth-Century United States* (Chicago: University of Chicago Press, 1962), p. 266.

91. Madison to Martin Van Buren, September 20, 1826, in Hunt (ed.), *Writings of Madison*, IX, 252–55.

92. Elazar, *The American Partnership*, pp. 32–33; Arthur Schlesinger, Jr., *The Age of Jackson* (Boston: Little, Brown & Co., 1945), pp. 33–34, 53.

93. Daniel Webster, speech of June 5, 1828, in *The Writings and Speeches of Daniel Webster* (18 volumes. Boston: Little, Brown, & Co., 1903), II, 17–20. The quotations are on pages 8 and 20.

94. Turner, *Rise of the New West*, pp. 291–92.

95. William MacDonald, *Jacksonian Democracy, 1829–1837* (New York: Harper & Bros., 1906), pp. 35–42.

96. Jackson to Monroe, July 26, 1822, in John S. Bassett (ed.), *Correspondence of Andrew Jackson* (7 volumes. Washington, D.C.: Carnegie Institution, 1926–1935), III, 171.

97. *Annals of Congress*, 18 Cong., 1 Sess., *passim.* Also see Marquis James,

The Life of Andrew Jackson (Indianapolis: Bobbs-Merrill Co., 1938), p. 393, and Edward Channing, *A History of the United States* (6 volumes. New York: Macmillan Co., 1905-1925), V, 321.

98. Jackson to James W. Lanier, [May 15?], 1824, in Bassett (ed.), *Jackson Correspondence*, III, 253. Also see Thomas P. Abernethy, *From Frontier to Plantation in Tennessee: A Study in Frontier Democracy* (2d ed., University: University of Alabama Press, 1967), pp. 244-45.

99. Schlesinger, *The Age of Jackson*, pp. 58-59.

100. Jackson to Col. Charles P. Tutt, June 30, 1827, in Bassett (ed.), *Jackson Correspondence*, III, 369.

101. The draft of Jackson's first inaugural address is in *ibid.*, IV, 10-13. The address as given is in Richardson (comp.), *Messages and Papers*, II, 437.

102. Richardson (comp.), *Messages and Papers*, II, 451-52. For the draft of the message see Bassett (ed.), *Jackson Correspondence*, IV, 102-103.

103. Jackson to John C. Overton, December 31, 1829, in Bassett (ed.), *Jackson Correspondence*, IV, 109.

104. *Writings of Webster*, XIV, 137-38.

105. Claude M. Fuess, *Daniel Webster* (2 volumes. Boston: Little, Brown, & Co., 1930), I, 362.

106. Webster, "Second Speech on Foot's Resolution," January 26, 1830, in *Writings of Webster*, VI, 22-35. The quotations are on page 35.

107. Clay, "Nullification and Other Topics" speech, August 3, 1830, in Colton (ed.), *Works of Clay*, VII, 413-14. The National Road as originally built in Indiana was equally primitive. See R. Carlyle Buley, *The Old Northwest: Pioneer Period, 1815-1840* (2 volumes. Indianapolis: Indiana Historical Society, 1950), I, 463.

108. MacDonald, *Jacksonian Democracy*, p. 139.

109. *Congressional Debates*, 22 Cong., 2 Sess., 820ff.

110. *Ibid.*, 21 Cong., 1 Sess., 433-35, 820-42.

111. Turner, *The United States*, pp. 390-91.

112. John C. Fitzpatrick (ed.), *Autobiography of Martin Van Buren* (American Historical Association *Annual Report, 1918*, Washington, D.C.: Government Printing Office, 1920), pp. 321-22. Also see Jackson's notes for the Maysville Road veto in Bassett (ed.), *Jackson Correspondence*, IV, 137-39 (especially p. 137n). Richardson (comp.), *Messages and Papers*, II, 483-93 is the veto as presented to Congress.

113. Bray Hammond, *Banks and Politics in America from the Revolution to the Civil War* (Princeton, N.J.: Princeton University Press, 1967), p. 352.

114. Fitzpatrick (ed.), *Van Buren Autobiography*, pp. 323-27.

115. Richardson (comp.), *Messages and Papers*, II, 483-93. For a summary and an analysis see Taylor, *The Transportation Revolution*, p. 20.

116. Richardson (comp.), *Messages and Papers*, II, 493-94.

117. Williams, *The Contours of American History*, p. 240.

118. Capers, *John C. Calhoun*, p. 126.

119. Elazar, *The American Partnership*, p. 306. Also see William W.

Freehling, *Prelude to Civil War: The Nullification Controversy in South Carolina, 1816–1836* (New York: Harper & Row, 1966), pp. 199–200.

120. Van Deusen, *The Jacksonian Era*, p. 52.

121. Taylor, *The Transportation Revolution*, p. 20.

122. Clay to Webster, June 7, 1830, in *Writings of Webster*, XVII, 504–505. Also see Webster to Clay, May 29, 1830, in Colton (ed.), *Private Correspondence of Clay*, pp. 274–75; Clay to J. S. Johnston, June 14, 1830, in *ibid.*, p. 278; and Clay to Francis Brooke, June 16, 1830, in *ibid.*, p. 279.

123. Clay to Adam Beatty, June 8, 1830, in Colton (ed.), *Private Correspondence of Clay*, p. 277.

124. Jackson to Van Buren, July 12, 1830, in Bassett (ed.), *Jackson Correspondence*, IV, 161. Also see Jackson to Major William B. Lewis, letters of June 21, 26, and 28, 1830, in *ibid.*, pp. 156–57.

125. Lee Benson, *The Concept of Jacksonian Democracy: New York as a Test Case* (Princeton, N.J.: Princeton University Press, 1961), p. 40.

126. Van Deusen, *The Jacksonian Era*, p. 52, and MacDonald, *Jacksonian Democracy*, p. 144.

127. Clay, "Nullification and Other Topics" speech, Cincinnati, August 3, 1830, in Colton (ed.), *Works of Clay*, VII, 408–14.

128. Madison to Van Buren, June 3, 1830, in Hunt (ed.), *Writings of Madison*, IX, 375–76. Also see Fitzpatrick (ed.), *Van Buren Autobiography*, p. 330.

129. Fitzpatrick (ed.), *Van Buren Autobiography*, pp. 330–35, which reprints letters of Madison and Van Buren, including Madison to Van Buren, July 5, 1830, which is also in Hunt (ed.), *Writings of Madison*, IX, 376–83.

130. Richardson (comp.), *Messages and Papers*, II, 508–17. Also see Jackson to Brig. Gen. John Coffee, December 28, 1830, in Bassett (ed.), *Jackson Correspondence*, IV, 216.

131. Thomas H. Benton, *Thirty Years View* (2 volumes. New York: D. Appleton & Co., 1854–1856), I, 26, 167.

132. Glyndon G. Van Deusen, *The Life of Henry Clay* (Boston: Little, Brown & Co., 1937), p. 238.

133. Eaton, *Henry Clay*, p. 110.

134. Clay to Francis Brooke, January 17, 1833, in Colton (ed.), *Private Correspondence of Clay*, p. 347.

135. Wheeler, *History of Congress*, II, 191. Also see Taylor, *The Transportation Revolution*, p. 21.

136. Alexander Johnston, *American Political History, 1763–1876* (2 volumes. New York: G. P. Putnam's Sons, 1905), I, 347.

137. U.S. *Statutes at Large*, IV, 681.

138. Nelson, "Presidential Influence in the Policy of Internal Improvements," in *Iowa Journal of History and Politics*, IV, 44, 52.

139. Stuart Bruchey, *The Roots of American Economic Growth, 1607–1861: An Essay in Social Causation* (New York: Harper & Row, 1965), pp. 133–34; Meyers, *The Jacksonian Persuasion*, pp. 113–14; and Turner, *The*

United States, pp. 312–13, 319–20. For the problems faced by one state see Esarey, *Internal Improvements in Indiana, passim.*

140. For a more favorable view of federal policy see Marcus Cunliffe, *The Nation Takes Shape, 1789–1837* (Chicago: University of Chicago Press, 1961), pp. 110–12.

141. Glyndon G. Van Deusen, "Some Aspects of Whig Thought and Theory in the Jacksonian Period," in *American Historical Review,* LXIII (1958), 315.

142. Dearing, *American Highway Policy,* pp. 34–35. Also see Taylor, *The Transportation Revolution,* pp. 20–21.

The Ohio River:
Pathway to Settlement

DONALD T. ZIMMER

In 1783, when the United States acquired claim to the trans-Appalachian West, a vast climax forest extending beyond the Mississippi River covered the entire area. Its sun-drenched top made an undulating ocean of leaves and branches seventy to eighty feet above ground level. Below, its shade made the land ponderously gloomy, but, more importantly, the forest's density obstructed overland travel, making westward movement time-consuming and difficult. The party that founded Nashville in 1779 floated down the Tennessee River and rowed and poled all the way up the adjacent Cumberland River, traveling at least eight hundred miles by water to avoid some two hundred miles by land. Even as late as 1829, when Andrew Jackson traveled by coach from Nashville to Washington, D.C., for his inauguration, it took the president-elect a solid month to make the journey. A verse inscribed in the register book of a tavern in Franklin, Indiana, recorded one sojourner's annoyance and frustration with land travel:

> The Roads are impassable—
> Hardly jackassable;
> I think those that travel 'em
> Should turn out and gravel 'em[1]

The only natural breaks in the forest were made by the numerous rivers and streams that dissected the region. In 1849 Major Stephen H. Long of the Topographical Engineers estimated that there were

---

Donald T. Zimmer is Professor of History in Tri-State University.

almost seventeen thousand miles of navigable rivers in the trans-
Appalachian West.[2] Nature had established a forest barrier to west-
ward settlement, but it also offered a means of breaking that barrier.
No river was more important to westward settlement than the Ohio.
Extending from the confluence of the Allegheny and the Monon-
gahela rivers at Pittsburgh to its mouth at Cairo, the Ohio River
stretched for over a thousand miles into the West. The Ohio River,
Charles Ambler has written, "is the main thoroughfare between the
Atlantic coast and the Mississippi valley. By way of its waters, more
than any other route, a whole continent was peopled."[3]

During the seasonal high water stages of spring and autumn, the
Ohio River appeared as a liquid pool extending from Pittsburgh to
Cairo. As high water receded, the river's most serious obstructions
appeared—the falls of the Ohio that separated the upper and lower
portions of the river and Letart's Rapids. The falls of the Ohio at
Louisville was a great ledge of limestone that fell about twenty-two
feet in a running distance of about three miles. Three channels or
chutes penetrated the rock ledge, but only the main one on the
Indiana side could be used with safety during periods of slack water.
At those times the roar of the water passing over the falls could be
heard half a mile away by boatmen descending the river. The
velocity of the current in these channels varied much of the year
between five and six miles an hour. Letart's Rapids, 234 miles below
Pittsburgh, was a rock ledge that fell about 3 feet in a running distance of half a mile. Current over the rapids ranged from four miles
per hour at low water to nearly six before high water submerged
them.[4]

Islands and bars or elevations in the riverbed of rock, gravel, and
sand were the most common obstacles to river navigation. Zadok
Cramer's *Navigator* listed 98 islands and Samuel Cumings's *Western
Pilot* listed 170 bars between Pittsburgh and the mouth of the Ohio.
The first hundred miles of the river were so full of these obstructions
that early immigrants and traders often preferred to trek across to
Wheeling to begin their downward voyage.[5] Ordinarily, sandbars
formed at the head and foot of each island, at the mouth of every
stream of any importance, and at many other places where the
slowing down of the current caused the water to deposit sand and silt.

Bars were at once both the plague of boatmen and the bene-
factors of navigation. They were a plague, since the depth of water

over the bars determined the seasons of navigation. Boatmen generally regarded about five to six feet of water in channels as a fair
stage for running and above forty feet as unsatisfactory, because
of the dangers of floating debris. The spring season of high water
and unrestricted navigation began with the breaking up of the ice
in February or March. The season of low water that restricted navigation usually began in the latter part of June and continued, only
briefly interrupted by occasional summer freshes, until the close of
September. The fall season of unrestricted navigation might last for
only two or three weeks or it might last for several months. Low
water and ice ended the fall season sometime between late November
and the first of January.[6]

Bars benefited navigation because they transformed the river into
what amounted to a natural slack-water system. These natural dams
created pools varying from half a mile to over fifteen miles in length,
and ten, fifteen, and more feet in depth. The current velocity in
these pools was a mile or less per hour. The bars, by creating these
pools, served two important functions for river navigation: they
prolonged the period of boating by retaining great quantities of
water that would otherwise rapidly run off; and they acted as a
brake, slowing the current of the surface water to about three miles
an hour, thereby making easier both downstream and especially
upstream navigation of the river.[7]

As the river meandered through the dense natural forest, the
force of its water created still another obstruction, the snag. Snags
were trees that fell into the river after the current had eroded away
the soil that had anchored them to the shore. The root end, being
least buoyant, usually became fixed in the riverbed, and normally
pointed downstream. These obstacles caused little problem for early
river craft like the flatboat and keelboat, but they were a serious
hazard for the steamboat. Before 1826, when the snag boat began to
clear the river effectively, snags accounted for the great majority
of steamboat losses. In nearly every instance, the damaged boat went
down within two to five minutes of the time of striking the snag.[8]

In the early years there were three principal points for downriver
embarkation: Pittsburgh (1760) and Brownsville (1785) in Pennsylvania, and Wheeling (1769) in Virginia. From these points many of
the pioneers began their journey down the Ohio River, and here also
boatbuilders constructed many of the early river craft. Flatboats,

keelboats, and barges were the pioneer vessels that first made settlement and survival possible. In use on the Ohio by 1780, flatboats, or "broadhorns," were simply great, oblong boxes without keel or modeling of the hull. They varied in length from twenty to one hundred feet, and from twelve to twenty feet in width. Depending on their size, a flatboat's carrying capacity ranged from thirty-five to two hundred tons. Boatmen steered the craft downstream with a thirty- or forty-foot oar pivoted in a fork stick fastened to the roof of the flatboat. Two or more sweeps, or broadhorns, pivoted on the sides were used to keep the boat in the current. Traveling as much as five miles an hour in flood water, these pioneer craft carried the main portion of downstream traffic and, even after the coming of the steamboat, remained the primary carrier of bulk goods.[9]

Keelboats and barges came into general use on the Ohio soon after the Revolution and remained for over thirty years the primary mode of upriver transportation. With the coming of the steamboat, their use receded from the trunk-line rivers to the shallower tributary rivers. Though it is difficult to draw sharp distinctions between the two types since both were long, narrow craft with sharp keels and well-modeled hulls, in general the keelboat was intended for shallow water, while the barge was built mainly for the deep water of the Mississippi and lower Ohio rivers. The ordinary keelboat was forty to eighty feet in length and seven to ten feet in beam. Sharp at both ends, it had a shallow keel drawing about two feet of water loaded. Burden ranged from between fifteen and fifty tons, but they usually carried less than thirty. On each side was a cleated footway, twelve to eighteen inches wide, and at the bow there were seats for four to twelve rowers. Boatmen steered by means of a long oar pivoted at the stern. Barges did not greatly exceed keelboats in length, but they varied from twelve to twenty feet in width. They ordinarily carried a cargo of forty tons or more, drawing three to four feet of water. They also differed from keelboats in that they always had a mast, often two, fitted with square sails, or rigged as a schooner, and were steered by a rudder. On the Ohio, winds blew most commonly from the south and southwest during the daytime, and by their aid a boat could ascend at the rate of two to five miles an hour.[10]

In order to avoid the full force of the current, boatmen kept ascending craft close to the shore in shallow water. The usual method of propelling both keelboats and barges was by setting poles that were about twenty feet in length. When the crew could not use poles or oars to move the boat, they used a cordelle, or towline, several hundred feet long. Where the bank was clear, men on shore pulled the boat by the towline. Where it was not, the crew fastened the towline to a snag, or tree, and drew up the boat either with a windlass or hand over hand. In this manner boatmen could travel upriver an average distance of about fifteen miles a day. The 1,950 miles from New Orleans to Pittsburgh took four months and more, while the return took four to six weeks.[11]

Supported by these early river craft, pioneer settlement advanced into the early Far West. All the early towns of the West, except Lexington, Kentucky, were founded on rivers. As spearheads of the frontier, towns began by gradually piercing their way into the forest lining the river banks, and their development was closely associated with the development of river transportation. Louisville began as a town in 1779 with settlers brought down the Ohio by George Rogers Clark. In 1778 he had embarked on the Ohio with 150 men and about 20 families of immigrants. Before setting off on his famous expedition to Kaskaskia, he settled these 20 families on Corn Island at the Falls of the Ohio, and the following spring they moved onto the mainland to found the town. Other towns soon followed. After the Revolution, a grateful Virginia granted Clark's men 150,000 acres of land on the north side of the Ohio opposite the falls, where settlement of Clarksville began in 1784. Four years later the Ohio Associates founded Marietta on the upper Ohio, and in the winter of 1788 a group of about twenty pioneers established a settlement opposite the mouth of the Licking River called Losantiville. The town's name, a curious combination of Greek, Latin, and French, was soon changed to Cincinnati.[12]

Through the remainder of the century and into the next, town settlement continued along the shores of the major and minor rivers. On the south shore of the Ohio in the Indiana Territory, Governor William Henry Harrison in 1802 urged the founders of the town of Jeffersonville to follow a plan recommended by Thomas Jefferson. Though the town did not follow Jefferson's unique pattern, it grew, and the national government established a land office there in 1808.[13] In that same year the first settlement was made on the site of Madison, a town that may serve as an illustration of the influence of the development of river transportation on town growth. John Wagoner, a tavern keeper from Chambersburg, Pennsylvania, and his wife had floated down the Ohio on a flatboat. They built the first cabin within the boundaries of the future town with the lumber from their boat.[14]

In 1808, the year the Wagoners built their cabin, John Paul and two others journeyed to the recently opened land office in Jeffersonville and purchased the 380 acres of bottomland on which the Wagoner cabin sat.[15] Paul was the son of Michael and Ann Paul, who had migrated with their children some time before the turn of the century from Germantown, Pennsylvania, to Brownsville. Probably moving by flatboat down the Ohio, the family lived for awhile in western Virginia before finally settling in Hardin County, Kentucky. As a young man, John Paul had moved in 1800, to Greene County, Ohio, where he operated a gristmill and served as clerk of the courts of the county until he made his journey to Jeffersonville. He probably returned to Greene County to wind up his affairs and dispose of his property, for it was then or perhaps earlier that he donated the land on which was located the town of Xenia, Ohio.[16]

In December, 1810, along with other proprietors, John Paul laid out the town of Madison. They chose the highest point above the second bank of the river and set the town out in a grid pattern of four blocks, sixteen squares of eight lots each.[17] During Madison's early years, when river traffic depended entirely on the flatboat and keelboat, the town made little progress. When John Melish visited Madison in the summer of 1811, the town contained three taverns, two general stores, two hatters, two blacksmiths, one brickmaker, and one stonemason. Melish reported twelve families living there in 1811,[18] but in 1814 a visitor found "there were eight or ten families in the town, not more." Until 1815, "the bottom [on which the village was located] was almost entirely covered with woods, only a little spot cleared for houses."[19] Main Street was the only street cleared of trees. The log cabins that comprised the village served as both homes and places of business.

Although Madison was little more than an embryo of settlement in 1811, a revolution in river transportation had begun that would transform it into a thriving river port. As early as 1785, James Rumsey in a letter to George Washington had expressed his conviction that "boats of passage may be made to go against the current of the Mesisipia or Ohio River . . . . from sixty to one hundred miles

American Heritage Publishing Company

This woodcut sketch of the first *New Orleans*, which was published in *Lloyd's Steamboat Directory*, 1856, inaccurately shows her as a stern-wheeler.

per day."[20] Easterners John Fitch, Oliver Evans, and Robert Fulton carried on their experiments with western rivers in mind. Fulton's *Clermont* was designed with the specific intention of use on the shallow water of western rivers.[21] Unfortunately, the deep-keeled, molded hull of the sailing ship, rather than the flat-bottomed, straight-sided hull of the *Clermont*, became the prototype of the early western steamboat.

Nicholas Roosevelt began building the first steamboat in the West, the *New Orleans*, at Pittsburgh in the spring of 1811. Constructed with a hull depth of twelve feet and carrying two masts, it was described as "built after the fashion of a ship." Surviving illustrations show her as both a side-wheeler and a stern-wheeler, but most authorities believe that, like the *Clermont*, she was a side-wheeler. The *New Orleans*'s maiden voyage began in October, 1811, and because of stopovers and delays took almost four months. It was not until the second week of January, 1812, that she arrived at New Orleans. Despite its slowness, this pioneer voyage encouraged the building and operation of other western steamboats. Within the next several years, half a dozen steamboats were plying western waters chiefly between Louisville and New Orleans. Nearly all of these early western steamboats measured less than one hundred tons and, because of their deep draft, were limited to the brief seasons of high water. Like the *New Orleans*, these early steamboats also resembled sailing ships with their deep keels, masts, bowsprits, and sails.[22]

Over the next several decades, boatbuilders, through a trial-and-error approach, changed the initial design of the sailing ship to conform to the needs of western river navigation. The short life-span—the average being about five years—and low cost of these vessels encouraged continual design and construction changes. Sails and masts disappeared after the first few years, as did the bowsprit, which had no function on a sailless boat. The bowsprit was replaced by the vertical jack staff, providing the pilot with a sight to aid steering. The steering wheel was brought forward and placed in a pilot house perched thirty, forty, or more feet above the main deck. Henry Shreve elevated the boilers and machinery from the hold to the main deck when he built the *Washington* in 1816. He added a third deck in 1825, permitting the accommodation of passengers in the upper between decks. Desiring buoyancy and light draft above

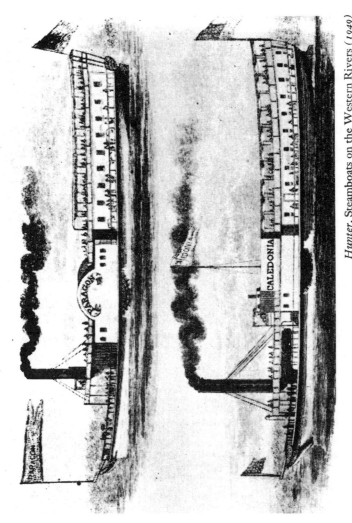

Hunter, Steamboats on the Western Rivers (*1949*)

The steamboats *Paragon* (1819) and *Caledonia* (1824)

all other qualities, steamboat builders made their most important change in the form and proportion of the hull. Builders stressed rectangular lines and flat surfaces, confining the curved surfaces of the hull largely within short distances from the bow and stern.[23]

Because of their limited numbers and concentration on the lower Ohio, the early river steamboats probably had little influence on the development of Madison. In 1817 the village only "contained about one hundred and fifty people" and the early settlers had made little improvement. "It was wholly without streets," wrote James F. D. Lanier in recalling his first arrival in Madison in 1817, "or any improvements fitted to make it an attractive or agreeable place."[24] Probably reflecting the town's dependence on the unwieldy flatboat and the infrequent keelboat, the settlement had no landing of any kind. "The original sycamore, cottonwood and willow trees," wrote an early settler, "were standing under and on the high bank; these grew out into the river, especially the cottonwoods."[25] A contributor to the *Indiana Republican* complained that the natural forest "so completely prevents a view of the town, to persons who are descending the river that many pass it before they are apprised of it;—or a view of the town breaks upon them so suddenly, that they cannot possibly effect a landing, particularly when the waters are high."[26] Even as late as 1833, so many trees still extended over the riverfront that the passing traveler had only an imperfect view of the town from the river.[27] The extensive clearing and development of the riverfront characteristic of Madison in its later years, came with expansion of steamboat commerce on the river.

The first great improvement in navigation on the Ohio River came with the building of a canal allowing all-season passage of boats around the falls at Louisville. A project for digging a canal was proposed as early as 1804, and a company was even chartered by the Indiana territorial assembly, but nothing came of the effort. In 1819 an Indiana company actually began construction, but work stopped when the builders discovered a large portion of the canal had to be cut through solid rock. Finally, a Kentucky corporation was formed in 1825 to build a canal on the south side of the falls. Work actually began in 1826, and the canal opened for traffic in December, 1830. Over four hundred steamboats and about the same number of other types of boats passed through the canal in its first year of operation. The annual number of steamboats passing through the canal passed the one thousand mark in 1835, and between 1835 and 1861 averaged about thirteen hundred steamboats a year.[28]

The importance of the canal to the expansion of steamboat operation is suggested by Table I. As the table indicates, only sixty-nine steamboats with a combined measured tonnage of 13,890 tons operated on all the western rivers in 1820. Only one of these, a small boat of 176 tons with a cargo capacity of perhaps no more than 90 tons, ran with any degree of regularity between Cincinnati and Louisville. Following the opening of the canal, the 1830s brought a boom in steamboat construction with the number of vessels increasing to 381 in 1836, and 536 by 1840. While the number reached its height in 1850 and thereafter declined, the measured tonnage did not.

TABLE I. Number and Tonnage of Steamboats Operating on the Western Rivers, 1817–1860.[29]

Year	Number	Tonnage	Year	Number	Tonnage
			1836	381	57,090
1817	17	3,290	1840	536	83,592
1820	69	13,890	1845	557	98,246
1823	75	12,501	1850	740	141,834
1825	73	9,992	1855	727	173,068
1830	187	29,481	1860	735	162,735

Prior to the opening of the canal, only two steamboats—the *General Pike* (1818–1825) and the *Ben Franklin* (1826–1833)—ran on anything like a schedule between Cincinnati and Louisville. The *General Pike* (176 tons) was a small boat with a carrying capacity of probably not much more than 90 tons. Though smaller, the *Ben Franklin* (163 tons), which replaced the *General Pike* in 1826, probably had a cargo capacity equal to her measured tonnage. Before the canal around the falls at Louisville opened, these boats would load at Cincinnati and ports downriver with passengers and cargo and reship at Louisville. There they would wait for the arrival of a New Orleans boat, then load for a return trip.[30] Since these steamboats made intermediate stops between Cincinnati and Louisville, discharging and receiving passengers and freight, they doubtless made occasional stops at Madison during these years. The frequent references in the Madison paper during these early years to steamboats "passing" rather than stopping suggest that even the regular

boats had little occasion to touch shore at Madison. "The beautiful
Steam Boat, *Gen. Pike*," reported the *Indiana Republican* in 1819,
"passed this place yesterday from Louisville, bound to Cincinnati."[31]

   That the observer viewed the *General Pike* as "beautiful" may
say more about the joy he found in the uniqueness of seeing a steamboat than about his aesthetic judgment. The top-heavy, boxlike
structure, the rectangular paddle-wheel housings, and the forward
and semidetached position of the chimneys of the early vessels hardly
justified characterizing them as "beautiful." The ungainly appearance of an early steamboat more rightly justified the humorist's
characterization of it as " 'an engine on a raft with $11,000 worth of
jig-saw work.' " Only as design changes of the steamboat increased
in the 1830s and 1840s did it assume the lines and proportions that
have made it a romantic symbol of the antebellum period. When
fully developed, many thought "the side-wheel river packet the
most beautiful creation of man."[32]

Kenneth M. Newman, The Old Print Shop
On June 30, 1870, the *Robert E. Lee* and the *Natchez* left New Orleans for Saint
Louis. In the contest, the *Robert E. Lee* reached Saint Louis over six hours ahead of
the *Natchez*.

The fully developed western steamboat had three decks: main, boiler, and hurricane. Each deck was recessed from the others, with the boiler deck usually the same width as the main deck below and with a promenade deck on the outer margin. Set back from the edge of the hurricane deck was a Texas, which was narrower than the main cabin and shorter in length. The Texas provided staterooms for the officers, with the pilothouse occupying only part of its width. Hull length increased from 220 to 250 feet for boats operating on the upper Ohio and from 240 to 270 feet for those used on the lower Ohio and the Mississippi. A few even reached 300 feet in length, but they were the exceptions. Guards commonly exceeding the width of the hull by 50 to 75 percent extended the deck beyond the line of the hull at the sides. The long, narrow, flat-bottomed, straight-sided, lightly constructed hull allowed the smaller class (300–600 tons) to run on 6.5 feet of water, while the length-to-depth ratio on all boats exceeded thirty to one. Paddle wheels grew to forty feet in diameter and eighteen feet in width, with the circular housing enclosing them reaching to and above the line of the hurricane deck. The use of two steam engines that averaged nearly 1,200 horsepower on medium-sized vessels made possible the larger paddle wheels. By the 1850s chimneys reached seventy-five to eighty-five feet and even ninety feet above the surface of the water.[33]

Design and construction changes improved the appearance of the steamboat, but more importantly, since the controlling objectives were buoyancy and speed, they enabled them to operate more economically by increasing both their cargo capacity and their speed. The first steamboats were so heavily constructed and equipped that builders consumed much of the boat's buoyancy in supporting the weight of vessel and machinery. The ratio of cargo capacity to tonnage measurement in such pioneer boats as the *General Pike* averaged about one to two.[34] As Table II indicates, by 1825 steamboats had a reported capacity of one ton of cargo to each measurement ton; by 1840, a ratio of one and one-half tons to one; and in the late forties occasionally a ratio of two to one.

Design advances also meant increases in speed. In 1811 the *New Orleans* moved at "the marvellous rate of nearly eight miles an hour," downriver.[35] Upriver, however, remained agonizingly slow for many years. In 1814 a steamboat passenger embarked for Cincinnati from Rising Sun, thirty-five miles below, and "such was the slow

TABLE II. Tonnage and Cargo Capacity of Typical Western Steamboats.[36]

Steamboat	Year Built	Measured Tonnage	Cargo Capacity (tons)
Philadelphia	1826	325	350
Factor	1838	173	250
Diamond	1842	308	450
Harry of the West	1843	490	750
Martha Washington	1847	299	600
United States	1847	33?	6,0
Sultana	1848	924	1,700
Uncle Sam	1848	741	1,300

speed of the steamer, that when he got to North Bend, he left the boat and walked to Cincinnati, arriving some twelve hours before the steamer."[37] Regardless of such instances, even the early steamboats were a marked improvement over the upstream travel time of the keelboat and barge. Ordinarily it took keelboat or barge from three to four months to make the journey from New Orleans to Louisville, with ten to twenty miles a day the average rate.[38] Pioneer steamboats in 1815 and 1817 made the trip in twenty-five days, though trips of thirty to thirty-five days were more usual. Such early steamboat travel on the river was done only during daylight hours, but as the art of navigation at night developed travel time declined. This, along with design changes, reduced the travel time from New Orleans to Louisville to ten days, thirteen hours in the 1820s; to seven days, six hours in the 1830s; and to five days, twelve hours in the 1840s. By the middle 1850s steamboats made regular port-to-port trips upstream at an average speed of about ten miles an hour and downstream from fourteen to sixteen miles an hour.[39]

Advances in carrying capacity and speed helped produce a steady decrease in steamboat freight rates. The downriver rate for goods shipped from Pittsburgh to Louisville declined from one dollar per hundred pounds in 1817 to 30 cents in 1833, and as low as 8 to 10 cents per hundred pounds for heavy goods in 1842. Upriver steamboat rates experienced a similar decline. In 1816 it cost four to five dollars per hundred pounds to ship goods from New Orleans to Louisville. By the early 1830s, following the opening of the canal around the falls, goods could be shipped from New Orleans to Louisville and Cincinnati for 62.5 cents per hundred pounds. In the winter of 1842–1843 a meeting of steamboatmen at New Orleans fixed rates for the trade from New Orleans to Louisville and Cincinnati at 25.0 cents per hundred pounds for heavy goods and 33.3 cents for groceries and merchandise.[40]

The improvement in carrying capacity and speed and the steady decrease in freight rates transformed Madison from primarily an entrepôt into a trading center, competing with Cincinnati and Louisville. In its early years the town served as a gateway for immigrants and goods to the interior of Indiana rather than as a shipping point. As Morris Birkbeck reported in 1817, such was the influx of strangers into Indiana "that the industry of the settlers is severely taxed to provide food for themselves, and a superfluity for new comers." He estimated it would be a number of years before a surplus would be produced for export.[41] Merchants made annual trips on horseback to Philadelphia and Baltimore, where they purchased goods that they received on the spring and fall rises of the river.[42] As an entrepôt, Madison remained largely a community of log structures, though the town paper reported that in 1825 "12 to 15 good buildings erected, mostly brick." With a population of about a thousand at this time, the town had some 180 dwellings, 24 stores—14 dry goods and 10 groceries—a market house, 2 taverns, 2 churches (Presbyterian and Methodist), a Masonic hall, and an academy. Its industries included two cotton spinning factories, a wool carding establishment, two oil mills, a rope factory, a gristmill, a steam mill, and a printing office.[43]

Not until the late 1820s did Madison begin to change from an entrepôt to a commercial trade center. As the town's hinterland developed, export of agricultural products became an important part of Madison's trade. In January, 1829, the *Indiana Republican* reported, "A considerable number of boats laden with pork, corn, flour, & C. & C. have departed from the landing at this place within a few weeks past for New Orleans, and many others are in a state of preparation soon to follow them." During the fall and winter of 1828–1829, traders shipped a greater quantity of produce from Madison than ever before.[44] Paralleling the growth of an agricultural export trade was the growth of an import trade that benefited from improvement in both the river and the steamboat. By the early 1830s steamboat freight rates had been so equalized for Madison that the *Indiana Republican* could report that goods could now be procured "on as good terms . . . here as at Cincinnati or Louisville."[45] The

Indiana Gazetteer reported in 1833 "that, within the months of March and April last, an amount not less than $120,000 in merchandise, was imported to this town [Madison], which was chiefly sold to country merchants at wholesale, on terms as fair as could be had at Cincinnati or Louisville."[46]

The transformation of Madison's riverfront mirrored the town's transition from an entrepôt to a commercial trade center. When John Paul sold the first lots in Madison, he envisioned that nothing more than one warehouse and one ferry house would ever be built between High Street and the river.[47] Probably not much more than this was built in the early years, for the town did not even have a floating wharf prior to 1830 when Paul died. "For many years past," wrote the editor of the *Indiana Republican* in the year of Paul's death, "the people of this place have labored under the disadvantage of not having a wharf of any kind opposite our town, on which passengers and goods from steamboats could be landed. Passengers have been much annoyed and goods sometimes injured by being landed in the mud."[48] The town obtained its first floating wharf "for the purpose of receiving and forwarding goods to and from the steamboats" in 1830 and its first permanent wharf in 1833.[49] In May of that year the town built a one hundred-foot wharf with a decline of eight inches in every ten feet of descent, at the foot of Main Street. The town constructed similar wharves at the foot of Mulberry Street in 1834, West Street in 1835, and East Street in 1836. These community-built port facilities remained the town's only wharves until 1845, when, in anticipation of completion of the Madison and Indianapolis Railroad, a private wharf was built at the bend of the track that ran along the first bank of the river. Thereafter, both private investors and the town government expanded Madison's wharves until, by 1851, they extended over most of the town's riverfront.[50]

An appreciation of how much the transformation of the riverfront affected Madison's commercial importance can be gained from one observer's description of the area as a veritable symphony of motion. Arrival and departure of the scheduled packets and the continual landing of boats of all sorts, "from a 'broadhorn' to a magnificent Mississippi 'floating palace,' together with the coming and going of the locomotives, with their trains, on the railroad, and the dashing to and fro of the drays, omnibusses, water-carts and other two and four-wheeled vehicles" made the riverfront a center of activity orchestrated by steamboat commerce.[51] On one day in the spring of 1851, ten steamboats—*St. Anthony* (184 tons), *Sea Gull* (149 tons), *Regulator* (155 tons), *Hoosier State* (343 tons), *Blue Wing* (170 tons), *Navigator* (154 tons), *Yorktown No. 2* (298 tons), *Mary Stephens* (229 tons), *Ben Franklin No. 8* (473 tons), and *Telegraph No. 2* (375 tons)—stood at Madison's several wharves receiving and discharging passengers and freight.[52]

After 1830, as Madison became an export center for the farm produce of its hinterland—particularly corn, wheat, and hogs—the town's food processing industries grew. John Paul built Madison's first gristmill behind the town on Crooked Creek in 1814.[53] No description exists of the mill, but it probably did not differ much from the other types of water-powered mills built in the state during this early period, i.e., a small affair operated by a water-powered turbine wheel that drove a single pair of burrs.[54] The mill served the needs of Madison until 1832, when two of its citizens built the town's first merchant mill. A large stone and frame structure, the mill stood five stories in height and had four pairs of steam-operated millstones that ground corn and wheat.[55] Between then and 1847, when Madison's railroad reached Indianapolis, two similar steam-operated mills were built, giving its milling industry the "capacity of grinding some eighteen hundred bushels of wheat per day."[56] In the next two years, two more steam-operated mills were built, the largest of which processed three hundred thousand bushels of wheat and processed seventy thousand barrels of flour in 1850.[57]

Madison's slaughtering and pork-packing industry followed a similar pattern of expansion. An advertiser in the *Western Eagle* in October, 1813, offered to buy hogs, presumably for "fatting" on corn and slaughtering; this is the first suggestion of such an industry. No clear indication appears, however, until 1819, when the *Indiana Republican* advertised "a place for slaughtering" hogs. While no figures exist to indicate the size of Madison's early pork industry, in 1828 one slaughterer advertised for one thousand hogs "delivered in Madison as early in November as the weather will admit to slaughter them."[58] Since the early slaughtering and packing processes were ordinarily separate industries, it is not known if packing was also done in Madison, but by 1830 the two were combined.[59] From then on, Madison's slaughtering and packing industry so expanded that it had hope of rivaling Cincinnati, the great "Pork-opolis" itself. During the years from 1836 to 1846, the number of hogs annually slaughtered and packed by Madison's butchers increased from fifteen thousand to sixty four thousand, and by the early 1850s exceeded one hundred and twenty thousand.[60] By then, Madison had three packing houses, the largest of which was the Mammoth Cave Pork House east of town on the Ohio River. The grounds of this packing house covered over eight acres, with an eleven-hundred-foot frontage on the river, "including a good wharf." Its buildings included "slaughtering, hanging, and packing houses, two stone warehouses, two large brick smoke houses, a brick lard rendering house, stable, sheds and paved pens, all of the most substantial quality."[61]

The growth of Madison reached its pinnacle in the early 1850s. In addition to milling and packing, the town boasted other processing industries, including breweries, lard renderers, candle and soap makers, bristle and curled hairbrush producers, and cooperage and tanning factories. A steamboat building industry, begun by James Howard in 1836, constructed twenty-three steamboats in the 1850s, ranging in size from the small *Quincy* (125 tons) to the luxurious *David White* (636 tons).[62] Madison's other industries included a railroad car works that manufactured freight, baggage, and passenger cars; an extensive iron foundry and steam engine manufactory that cast steam engine cylinders requiring as much as two-and-a-half tons of liquid metal per unit; and furniture factories and lumber mills. Business enterprises included numerous wholesale and retail merchants, eleven hotels, several insurance companies, and three banks. Twelve churches and five schools served the community's population of some eight thousand, many of whom lived in stately houses.[63]

The house of James F. D. Lanier surpassed all others in stateliness and size. Built in 1844, in the classical Greek mode by a Baltimore carpenter-architect, Francis Costigan, the mansion measured sixty-seven feet by fifty-four feet. The house was a brick structure three stories high built on a stone foundation with walls two-feet thick. On the south side, facing the river, Costigan built a portico twelve feet wide and fifty feet long. Four columns, measuring upwards of thirty feet in height and having Corinthian capitals, supported the roof.[64] Before leaving to continue his career in Indianapolis, Costigan

View of the city of Madison, Indiana

built other fine houses in Madison, including the Shrewsbury House. The contrast between Costigan's houses and the town's first log cabins suggests how much the town had prospered since its founding.

Much of this prosperity depended on the steamboat, and its fate determined the fate of Madison. Steamboat travel had always involved risk, but, when measured against the pace of the flatboat and keelboat, the advantages seemed worth it. Fire and explosion were the chief hazards on steamboats, but cholera was also exacerbated by steamboat travel since the infection was carried rapidly by travelers to the port cities they visited. The first major cholera epidemics occurred in the West in 1832, with recurring major epidemics in 1833, 1834, 1848, 1849, 1850, and 1854.[65] A contemporary of the cholera epidemic that struck Madison in 1833 described the effect the dread disease had on river towns when it struck: "To realize and appreciate the conditions and appearance of things here, during that period of horror and desolation," he wrote, "would be impossible except and only for those who were present and able to endure its terrors." Many fled the town to find shelter and safety with friends and acquaintances in the country. Those who remained stayed in their homes, nursing the sick and preparing the dead for burial. "Here and there, in the deserted streets, a few men might occasionally be seen talking in melancholy undertones, asking if this or that one, who had but an hour before been stricken, was still living?" The latest news having been obtained, they separated and returned to their homes, "strongly fearing that some of their loved ones had been attacked during their absence of a few moments." All the stores and shops of Madison closed under these conditions and "had every appearance of having been abandoned to their fate."[66] Cholera moved up and down the river, harbored in the filth and stench of the overcrowded deck quarters, endangering all who came in contact with the steamboat.

Though cholera was the steamboat's most dreaded scourge, fire and explosion were its chief hazards. Steamboats were particularly susceptible to fire because of the slight and flimsy construction of their superstructures and because they often carried combustible cargoes. Once started, fire spread rapidly, and, because few persons were able to swim, the only hope of preventing heavy casualties lay in getting the vessel to shore. This, however, was often impossible because fire would burn the hempen tiller ropes that ran much of the boat's length, causing loss of control. Boat fires even a few hundred feet from shore frequently caused heavy loss of life. In 1837 the *Ben Sherrod*, operating out of Louisville, went up in flames with a loss of life reported variously at 120 to 175 persons from among some 200 passengers.[67]

Probably because they were old and familiar calamities, steamboat fires attracted much less public attention and concern than did boiler explosions. This was not only because of the unexpected suddenness of the explosions and their devastating force, but also because they accounted for half of all loss of life in steamboat accidents. Boiler explosions occurred most frequently just as the steamboat was getting under way after a landing, when a good head of steam was needed to overcome inertia, rather than when it was driving at full speed between ports. Fully two thirds of the major disasters by explosion on the western rivers before 1852 took place as the boat left the bank, or, in a few instances, while it remained at a landing.[68] In 1838 the *Moselle* left the city wharf at Cincinnati and proceeded upriver about a mile to pick up waiting passengers at a suburb. Just as the vessel cast loose from its mooring after having taken on the waiting passengers, three of its four boilers exploded with a tremendous roar. Although it is not known with certainty, probably at least 150 of the 280 passengers lost their lives.[69]

Throughout the country newspapers carried the stories of steamboat disasters and the risks of steamboat travel. The stories made a deep impression on the public mind but in themselves did not bring on the decline of steamboat travel as long as no viable alternative existed. The railroad at first did not appear to be an alternative, but rather a supplement, to river transportation. Most boatmen and many others thought of the railroad not as a competitor but as a feeder to the trunk routes of the Ohio and Mississippi rivers. Even the *American Railroad Journal* reflected this view when it wrote in 1850, "No artificial highway is likely to compete with the Father of Waters; for even with every facility for making railroads, it is not probable that the western people can ever reduce freights on their roads to less than 1 cent per ton per mile."[70]

Costs were only one transportation consideration and often not the most important. For passengers, speed and punctuality were often more important than cost or comfort. In this respect, railroads had the advantage because steamboats could not match railroads for speed, and punctuality on rivers was rare. While the distance between Cincinnati and Pittsburgh was 470 river miles compared to 316 rail miles, the travel time between the two river ports by steamboat was three days, six hours, versus fifteen hours by railroad for passengers and thirty-six hours for freight. As indicated in Table III, similar travel time advantages existed for the railroad over steamboats for all the major port cities. Since speed ordinarily was more important to passengers than shippers, steamboats first felt the effect of railroad competition in passenger business.

TABLE III. Typical Trip Times by Steamboat and Railroad in Late 1850s[71]

	Steamboat (Passengers and Freight)	Railroad	
		Passenger	Freight
Cincinnati to:			
Pittsburgh	3 days, 6 hours	15 hours	36 hours
St. Louis	2 days, 22 hours	16 hours	30 hours
New Orleans	8 days	60 hours	
Louisville to:			
Cincinnati	15 hours	7 hours	12 hours
Pittsburgh	4 days	22 hours	48 hours
St. Louis	2 days, 12 hours	14 hours	24 hours

Low freight charges were the only advantage the steamboat had over the railroad and then only during seasons of unrestricted navigation. Drought and low water particularly plagued the West in the 1850s and made its travelers railroad minded. "I cannot say," steamboat Captain E. Bennet wrote in 1870, "that the boats have been stopped by low water more than in the summer of 1854 and 1856. In 1854, our boats were laid by 82 days, and a good part of that time there was no navigation for any steamboat of lighter draught (our boats draw 3 feet light)."[72] In 1856 drought delayed the fall rise until about December 5, and then freezing weather began within two weeks, completely closing the river with ice by December 24. Navigation did not begin again until February 7, 1857. The "freeze-up" of 1854 lasted even longer, until March 6, 1855. The sequence of low water and ice in the 1850s recalled to many John Randolph's opposition to improvement of the Ohio on the grounds that "it was frozen over one half the year and dry the other half."[73]

As the river depths declined and navigation became restricted, the margin between railroad and steamboat rates disappeared. " 'They are the same as steamboat rates' " became a familiar phrase associated with railroad rates during the seasons of low water.[74]

The natural advantages of the railroad and the disadvantages of the steamboat combined in the 1850s to bring on the decline of steamboat navigation on the western rivers. The first important invasion by the railroad of the western steamboat's territory was the rail connection established between Pittsburgh and Cincinnati in the early fifties. The Ohio and Pennsylvania Railroad, chartered in 1848, completed a line to its western terminal at Crestline, nearly two hundred miles from Pittsburgh in the spring of 1853. An already completed line from there to Cincinnati linked the two leading ports of the upper Ohio River. For the first time, western steamboats faced direct main-line competition. The following January, rail connections by way of Chicago linked Cincinnati and Saint Louis. By the summer of 1854, the Ohio and Mississippi Railroad established rail service between Cincinnati and Louisville. The Ohio Central Railroad, completed in November, 1854, gave Cincinnati a second direct rail route to the East, via Columbus to Wheeling and the Baltimore and Ohio Railroad. The completion of the Ohio and Mississippi Railroad between Cincinnati and Saint Louis in 1857, provided fast, reliable, and direct main-line competition over the entire length of the Ohio River. Within a few years, the railroad had "relegated steamboats to a minor role in the economic life of the West."[75]

Madison derived much of its importance, as Edmund Dana wrote in 1819, "from its central position, by standing in one of the most northerly bends of the Ohio; thereby presenting one of the nearest points of Ohio navigation to that extensive body of rich land, at and around the Delaware towns, which yet remained uncultivated."[76] As a river port through which commerce moved to and from the Ohio "to that extensive body of rich land," Madison's fortunes were tied intimately with the condition of river commerce. The challenge of the railroad meant the decline of Madison as a center of industry and commerce. The ledger of the Mercantile Agency of New York listed some three hundred businesses as having gone out of existence there between 1844 and 1860. Fewer than a hundred of these disappeared in the nine years prior to 1852, while more than a hundred and sixty of them went out of business in the five years between 1853 and 1857.[77] Big as well as small businesses failed during this period. The bankruptcy of David White in 1856 represented an all-too-common occurrence. In better times the editor of the Madison *Daily Courier* regularly referred to White as "Old Enterprise" because of the many business activities in which he engaged. In addition to his many corporate interests, White owned steamboats, including the *Western World* and the *David White*, real estate in Madison valued at eighteen thousand dollars, and the Mammoth Cave Pork House that dressed 51,192 hogs in the 1850–1851 packing season. In 1852 the Mercantile Agency's reporter in Madison estimated him to be worth at least two hundred and fifty thousand dollars. White had come to Madison in the late 1840s and remained there until he went broke. When he left Madison, he moved to Keokuk, Iowa, still placing his faith in the future of river commerce. In 1861 the credit reporter for the Mercantile Agency in Keokuk succinctly reported White's credit as "utterly worthless" and in 1862 simply advised, "strike him out."[78]

In surveying the economic havoc of the Panic of 1857, the editor of the Madison *Courier* observed "some consolation, in these hard times, in the fact that Madison has not been a fast city during the last half decade; having been on our backs so long, we are used to it, and it enables us to see the stars falling around us."[79] Calvin Fletcher wrote of Madison in 1854 that "it has had its best days"; he might also have added that so, too, had western steamboat commerce.[80] By providing low-cost transportation, the western steamboat had done much to stimulate both settlement and economic development of the West. In his classic study of the western steamboat, Louis C. Hunter observed:

> Without the steamboat the advance of the frontier, the rise of cities, the growth of manufacturing, and the emancipation of an agricultural people from the drab confines of a frontier economy would all have taken place, but they would have been slowed to the tempo of keelboat, flatboat, and canal barge and to the tedious advance of stagecoach and wagon train. The growth of the West and the rise of steamboat transportation were inseparable; they were geared together and each was dependent upon the other.[81]

NOTES

1. J. C. Furnas, *The Americans: A Social History of the United States, 1587–1914* (New York: G. P. Putnam's Sons, 1969), pp. 252, 265–66; Ralph D. Gray (ed.), *The Hoosier State* (2 volumes. Grand Rapids, Mich.: William B. Eerdmans Publishing Co., 1981), I, 157.

2. Louis C. Hunter, *Steamboats on the Western Rivers: An Economic and Technological History* (Cambridge, Mass.: Harvard University Press, 1949), p. 217.

3. Charles Henry Ambler, *A History of Transportation in the Ohio Valley* (Glendale, Calif.: Arthur H. Clark Co., 1932), p. 17.

4. Hunter, *Steamboats on the Western Rivers*, pp. 226, 233.

5. Zadok Cramer, *The Navigator* (6th ed. Pittsburgh: Published by the author, 1808); Samuel Cumings, *The Western Pilot* (rev. ed. Cincinnati: G. Conclin, 1838); Leland D. Baldwin, *The Keelboat Age on Western Waters* (Pittsburgh: University of Pittsburgh Press, 1941), p. 71.

6. W. Milnor Roberts, "Survey of the Ohio River" (1870), U.S. *House Executive Documents*, 41 Cong., 3 Sess., No. 72, p. 24.

7. Hunter, *Steamboats on the Western Rivers*, pp. 231–32.

8. *Ibid.*, p. 235.

9. Baldwin, *The Keelboat Age on Western Waters*, pp. 47–50.

10. *Ibid.*, pp. 44–45.

11. *Ibid.*, p. 66.

12. Richard C. Wade, *The Urban Frontier, 1790–1830* (Cambridge, Mass.: Harvard University Press, 1959), pp. 14–15, 22–23; John W. Reps, *The Making of Urban America* (Princeton, N.J.: Princeton University Press, 1965), pp. 222–25.

13. Reps, *The Making of Urban America*, pp. 317–19; Howard H. Peckham, *Indiana: A History* (New York: W. W. Norton & Co., 1978), p. 39.

14. *Biographical and Historical Souvenir for the Counties of Clark, Crawford, Harrison, Floyd, Jefferson, Jennings, Scott and Washington* (Chicago: John M. Gresham & Co., 1889), pp. 184, 213.

15. Jeffersonville Land Office, Register of Certificates, 1808–1816, Registration No. 105, Archives Division, Commission on Public Records, Indiana State Library and Historical Building.

16. *Biographical and Historical Souvenir for the Counties of Clark, Crawford, Harrison, ...*, p. 203; George F. Robinson, *History of Greene County, Ohio* (Chicago: S. J. Clarke Publishing Co., 1902), p. 38.

17. Testimony of John Vawter, auctioneer at first sale of town lots, *Trustees of the City of Madison v. John Paul et al.*, Jefferson Circuit Court Record, July 24, 25, and August 16, 22, 1833, typescript, Jefferson County Library, Madison, Indiana, p. 5.

18. John Melish, *Travels in the United States of America, in the Years 1806 and 1807, and 1809, 1810, 1811* (2 volumes. Philadelphia, 1812), II, 142.

19. John Burns quoted in Grace Vawter Bicknell, *The Vawter Family in*

America (Atlanta, Ga.: Thorpe & Assoc., 1969), p. 388. James F. D. Lanier recalled when he arrived in 1817, "The town . . . was still a forest—the trees that were not standing almost covered the ground where they fell." *Sketch of the Life of J.F.D. Lanier* (2d ed. New York, 1877), p. 11.

20. Hunter, *Steamboats on the Western Rivers*, p. 6.

21. *Ibid.*, p. 66.

22. *Ibid.*, pp. 15–16, 67–68, 101.

23. *Ibid.*, pp. 61–105 *passim.*

24. *Sketch of the Life of J.F.D. Lanier*, p. 11.

25. James B. Lewis, "The Pioneers of Jefferson County," in *Indiana Magazine of History*, XII (1916), 215.

26. Madison *Indiana Republican*, December 20, 1817.

27. *The Indiana Gazetteer* (Indianapolis: Douglass and Maguire, 1833), p. 111.

28. Hunter, *Steamboats on the Western Rivers*, pp. 182–84.

29. *Ibid.*, p. 33.

30. Jonathan H. Baker to Captain E. W. Gould, November 28, 1888, in Emerson W. Gould, *Fifty Years on the Mississippi, or Gould's History of River Navigation* (St. Louis: Nixon-Jones Printing Co., 1889), p. 377.

31. Madison *Indiana Republican*, March 13, 1819.

32. Hunter, *Steamboats on the Western Rivers*, p. 171.

33. *Ibid.*, pp. 91–93.

34. *Ibid.*, p. 82.

35. Archer Butler Hulbert, *The Ohio River: A Course of Empire* (New York: G. P. Putnam's Sons, 1906), p. 331.

36. Hunter, *Steamboats on the Western Rivers*, p. 652.

37. Rev. B. F. Morris, *Historical Sketch of Rising Sun, Indiana. . . . Delivered September 15, 1856* (Cincinnati: Moore, Wilstach, Keys & Co., 1858).

38. Baldwin, *The Keelboat Age on Western Waters*, p. 66.

39. Hunter, *Steamboats on the Western Rivers*, pp. 17–19, 22–24.

40. *Ibid.*, pp. 25–27; Thomas S. Berry, *Western Prices before 1861: A Study of the Cincinnati Market* (Cambridge, Mass.: Harvard University Press, 1943), pp. 43–65; James Mak and Gary M. Walton, "Steamboats and the Great Productivity Surge in River Transportation," in *Journal of Economic History*, XXXII (September, 1972), 619–40.

41. Morris Birkbeck, *Notes on a Journey in America, from the Coast of Virginia to the Territory of Illinois* (Dublin, 1818), p. 93.

42. Madison *Evening Courier*, October 26, 1883.

43. Mary Hill (ed.), "Typescript Copy of Articles from Early Issues of Madison Newspapers" (Madison, Ind., Jefferson County Library, n.d.).

44. Madison *Indiana Republican*, January 14, 1829.

45. *Ibid.*, April 21, 1831.

46. *Indiana Gazetteer* (1833), p. 111.

47. Testimony of John Vawter, *Trustees of the City of Madison v. John Paul*, p. 3.

48. Madison *Indiana Republican*, March 3, 1830.

49. *Ibid.*, February 17, 1830; entry dated May 7, 1833, City of Madison, Town Record, April, 1824, to April, 1833, Clerk Treasurer's Office, City Hall, Madison, Indiana.

50. Entries dated April 1, 1834, June 12, 1835, and January 1, 1836, Madison Town Record; Madison *Weekly Courier*, June 21, 1845; Madison *Daily Courier*, May 12, 1851.

51. Madison *Daily Courier*, November 6, 1850.

52. Madison *Daily Tribune*, April 16, 1851.

53. Bicknell, *The Vawter Family*, p. 388.

54. George Branson, "Early Flour Mills in Indiana," in *Indiana Magazine of History*, XXII (1926), 23–24.

55. Madison *Indiana Republican*, July 19, 1832.

56. Madison *Weekly Courier*, September 11, 1847.

57. United States Census of Manufacturing, 1850, Archives Division, Commission on Public Records, Indiana State Library and Historical Building.

58. Madison *Western Eagle*, October 22, 1813; Madison *Indiana Republican*, December 25, 1819, and October 15, 1828.

59. Rudolf Alexander Clemen, *The American Livestock and Meat Industry* (New York: Ronald Press Co., 1923), p. 124; Madison *Indiana Republican*, November 25, 1830.

60. W. G. Lyford, *The Western Address Directory, 1837* (Baltimore: J. Robinson, 1837), p. 339; Madison *Weekly Courier*, January 31, 1846; Madison *Daily Courier*, January 15, 1853.

61. Madison *Daily Courier*, July 5, 1856.

62. Madison *Republican and Banner*, June 1, 1836; William M. Lytle, *Merchant Steam Vessels of the United States, 1807–1868* "*The Lytle List*," edited by Forrest R. Holdcamper (Mystic, Conn.: Steamship Historical Society of America, 1952).

63. *Williams' Madison Directory, City Guide, and Business Mirror*, Volume I, 1859–1860, compiled by C. S. Williams (Madison, Ind.: W. P. Levy & Co., 1859).

64. Madison *Republican and Banner*, November 27, 1844.

65. Hunter, *Steamboats on the Western Rivers*, p. 431.

66. Madison *Evening Courier*, November 7, 1883.

67. Hunter, *Steamboats on the Western Rivers*, pp. 277–80.

68. *Ibid.*, p. 295.

69. *Ibid.*, p. 285.

70. *American Railroad Journal*, May 4, 1850, p. 274.

71. Hunter, *Steamboats on the Western Rivers*, p. 490.

72. Quoted from W. Milnor Roberts, "Survey of the Ohio River" (1870), U.S. *House Executive Documents*, 41 Cong., 3 Sess., No. 72, p. 23.

73. Ambler, *A History of Transportation*, pp. 204–205.

74. Hunter, *Steamboats on the Western Rivers*, p. 493.

75. *Ibid.*, p. 481.

76. Edmund Dana, *Geographical Sketches on the Western Country* (Cincinnati: Looker, Reynolds & Co., 1819), pp. 118–19.

77. Credit Reporting Ledgers of the Mercantile Agency, Indiana, Jefferson County, 1884–1889, Volume 50, pp. 389–400, Baker Library, Harvard Business School, Boston.

78. Credit Reporting Ledger, p. 27, *ibid.*; Madison *Weekly Courier*, June 21, 1848; Madison *Daily Courier*, January 14, 1851; Credit Reporting Ledger for the Mercantile Agency, Iowa, Lee County, 1847–1879, Volume 25, p. 127, Baker Library, Harvard Business School, Boston.

79. Madison *Daily Courier*, October 16, 1857.

80. Gayle Thornbrough *et al.* (eds.), *The Diary of Calvin Fletcher* (8 volumes to date. Indianapolis: Indiana Historical Society, 1972—), V, 281.

81. Hunter, *Steamboats on the Western Rivers*, p. 32.

The Canal Era in the Old Northwest

RONALD E. SHAW

Our mode of travel exerts such a hold on popular imagination that we have often made it a symbol for an age. So it has been with the canal era in the United States. Today the canals of the Old Northwest have particular fascination because of the great distances dug into artificial waterways, the accomplishments of human muscle and self-taught engineers, the application of public enterprise, and the distinctive flavor imparted to life on the canals and in the towns that grew up beside them.[1]

Our account might begin with the Louisville and Portland Canal at the falls of the Ohio at Louisville, even if built on the Kentucky side and not strictly part of the Old Northwest. A company was chartered for the purpose in Indiana as early as 1805, and construction actually began in Indiana in 1819. Cincinnatians were deeply involved in the Kentucky venture, and when the canal was finished in 1830 it was vital to the steamboat traffic on the Ohio so central in the development of the Old Northwest.[2]

This canal and those built in Ohio, Indiana, Illinois, and Michigan were responses to the Erie Canal in New York which was begun in 1817 and finished in 1825. Canal movements in the Old Northwest sought either to share in the opportunity offered by a navigable waterway from Lake Erie to the Hudson or to emulate the success of the Erie Canal.

In 1818 Governor Ethan Allen Brown of Ohio urged the Ohio legislature to begin surveys from Lake Erie to the Ohio River. The

---

Ronald E. Shaw is Professor of History in Miami University of Ohio.

survey law of 1822 was the work of a committee headed by Micajah
Williams of Cincinnati, a city which was dependent upon an unpre-
dictable New Orleans market, but at the same time was opposed to a
canal in eastern Ohio. Five routes between Lake Erie and the Ohio
were proposed, and a canal commission was delegated for a selection.
Two engineers, James Geddes and David Bates, came from New
York to survey, and Alfred Kelley of Cleveland and Micajah Williams served as acting commissioners They inspected the Erie Canal,
made surveys themselves, shrewdly compromised urban and regional
rivalries, and secured legislative approval for two canals in 1825.[3]
One would take an eastern and central path, and the other would be
built in the southwest corner of the state. De Witt Clinton himself
came in 1825 to break ground, first south of Newark for the Ohio
and Erie Canal, and then at Middletown for the Miami Canal.

The Ohio and Erie Canal combined parts of two routes: the
northern portion of a Cuyahoga-Muskingum line, and the Scioto
Valley in the south, which had been part of a more central Scioto-
Sandusky route. Beginning at Cleveland, the canal ran up the Cuyahoga Valley to the Portage summit at Akron, followed the Tusca-
waras Valley and crossed the Walhonding River at Roscoe, crossed
the Licking summit, and with a feeder to Columbus met the Scioto
River as it flowed to the Ohio River at Portsmouth. The second
canal, the Miami Canal, began at Cincinnati and ran up the Miami
Valley to Dayton, later to be extended to Lake Erie.

Modeled on the Erie Canal, these canals were forty feet wide
and four feet deep, with locks of ninety feet by fifteen feet—tiny
dimensions to the modern eye but stupendous then. Ohio also copied
the New York practice of construction supervised by canal commissioners, while financing was managed by the commissioners of
the Canal Fund. This understaffing for so great a public enterprise
left much to personal endeavor.[4] Money was raised in New York,
and by 1828 the sixty-six-mile Miami Canal with its fifty-four locks
was completed at a cost of $900,000. The Ohio and Erie Canal, 333
miles with 152 locks and 14 aqueducts, was finished in 1834. Its $4.3
million cost was less than any other of like mileage in America.[5]

As with almost every state that built canals, the greatest threat
to the Ohio canals lay in the prospect of their own success, which
would lead to a large number of new canals in the state. New
canals were approved in 1836, and the "Loan law" of 1837 allowed

Wilcox, The Ohio Canals
(*Kent State Univ. Press, 1969*)

The Ohio canals

public funds to be loaned to private companies in what Harry N. Scheiber has called a policy of "mixed enterprise."[6] The costly Miami Extension Canal was opened in 1845, north from Dayton to the St. Mary's summit and following the Auglaize and Maumee valleys to join the Wabash and Erie Canal near Defiance, with its terminus at Toledo.[7] In the southwest extremity of Ohio, the Cincinnati and Whitewater Canal was completed by a private company in 1843. This remarkable canal crossed the Miami River on an aqueduct, tunneled through a ridge, and connected to Indiana's

Whitewater Canal. At Middletown on the Miami Canal, the short-lived Warren County Canal ran east to Lebanon.

Turning now to eastern Ohio, three lateral canals and the canalization of the Muskingum River created new connections to the Ohio River. The Muskingum was canalized from Marietta to Zanesville, and a canal added to join the Ohio and Erie at Dresden Junction was finished in 1841. The Hocking Valley Canal was added in 1843, leaving the Ohio and Erie at Carroll and continuing fifty six miles through the coal and salt mining region to Athens. Above these southeasterly laterals, the Walhonding Canal, running for twenty-five miles northwest from Roscoe up the Walhonding Valley toward the agricultural center of the state, opened in 1841.

In northeastern Ohio, two more canals struck out for the shortest routes to the Ohio River and the Pennsylvania canals. The Sandy and Beaver, requiring seventy-three miles from Bolivar on the Ohio and Erie to East Liverpool on the Ohio, was under private construction for five years and was finished in 1848. Farther north, the Pennsylvania and Ohio Canal (often called the Mahoning Canal) was built by a private company aided by the state. The section of the canal leaving the Ohio and Erie at Akron and passing through Warren and Youngstown to the Ohio line was completed in 1839, while the Pennsylvania portion was finished to Pittsburgh the next year. On Lake Erie the Milan Canal extended only three miles from the lake port of Huron to Milan in the wheat-growing region. When it was opened, built by a state-assisted company, it made Milan a great interior wheat port.

Altogether, Ohio had almost eight hundred miles of canals, built at a cost of more than $15 million.[8] With some exceptions, the trade, if not the canal tolls, envisioned by their planners was largely realized. Wheat arriving at Cleveland in 1851 reached 2,529,699 bushels for that year alone; flour, 645,730 barrels; corn, 998,059 bushels; coal, 2,992,342 bushels; while nearly 11 million pounds of merchandise cleared Cleveland for inland distribution. Moving south in 1851, canal trade arriving at Portsmouth included 403,094 bushels of corn; wheat, 70,430 bushels; flour, 49,802½ barrels; and pork and bacon, 4,679,759 pounds; while 2,604,084 pounds of merchandise moved north up the canal.[9]

The Miami and Erie Canal was less heavily used than the Ohio and Erie, but its trade was a major boost in the rise of Cincinnati as the Queen City. In 1851 the canal brought to Cincinnati 130,292 bushels of wheat; flour, 317,107 barrels; and corn 270,147 bushels. In all but three years from 1833 to 1850, between 18,000 and 35,000 barrels of pork came to Cincinnati by the Miami Canal, while almost 9.5 million pounds of merchandise cleared the canal in 1846 and more than 6 million pounds in 1851.[10] But railroad competition brought a rapid decline thereafter. Canal tolls, balanced against expenses, were disappointing.[11] The Ohio canals did not yield the wealth anticipated following the success of the Erie Canal in New York, nor did they reverse the direction of western Ohio trade from New Orleans.

Since the Indiana canals are the subject of another paper in this symposium, only brief summaries of them will be given here. Indiana built the longest canal in the early nation, the 468-mile-long Wabash and Erie Canal, beginning with an Ohio portion at Toledo and crossing the summit near Fort Wayne between the Wabash and Maumee to go on to Evansville on the Ohio River. Begun at Fort Wayne in 1832, it reached Peru in 1837, Lafayette in 1843, Terre Haute in 1848, and Evansville in 1853. As in other western states, the canals in Indiana depended on national land grants. In 1827 when a grant was given to aid the Illinois and Michigan Canal, a donation was also given to Indiana.[12] As in Ohio, regional rivalry existed in Indiana; the Whitewater Canal in the southeastern corner of Indiana from Lawrenceburg to Brookville and above was a constant competitor for state funds.[13]

But a more important supplement to the Wabash and Erie was the ill-fated Central Canal, of which only a short portion through Indianapolis was ever fully completed. Leaving the Wabash and Erie at Peru, its route was to swing southeast to Marion, then south to Indianapolis, through Martinsville and Spencer to Worthington, where it would connect with an extension from the Wabash and Erie. The Wabash and Erie Canal left the Wabash River at Terre Haute, took a "cross-cut" to Worthington, and finally followed the route of the Central Canal to Evansville. In this grand scheme an eastern branch of the Central Canal from Anderson to Muncietown would link up with the Whitewater Canal.

After the land grant, Indiana was confronted with a decision similar to that being faced in Philadelphia, Baltimore, and Boston in their rivalry with the Erie Canal: whether to build a canal or try the unproven technology of the railroad.[14] In 1832 Indiana's decision

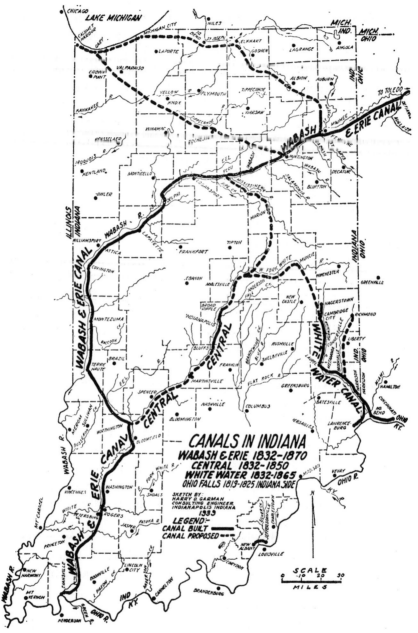

Garman, The Whitewater Canal (1944)

went to the more conservative choice of a canal, and the familiar prism for the canal era was adopted, forty feet wide and four feet deep. Indiana's Board of Public Works and Board of Fund Commissioners resembled that of Ohio but demonstrated grievous deficiencies in operation.[15]

The Indiana canals were launched in the period of canal enthusiasm that came to be known as the "canal mania." The "Mammoth Bill" of 1836 authorized $10 million to be borrowed for a vastly expanded system, in which work would begin on all projects at the same time. When the Panic of 1837 struck and the state's credit was hurt by the failure of the Morris Canal and Banking Company, the Wabash and Erie was financed by state scrip and by another congressional land donation made to both Ohio and Indiana. Canal navigation was opened from Lafayette to Toledo in 1843, and the Whitewater Canal reached north from Lawrenceburg to Cambridge City in 1846.[16]

The state was insolvent after 1841. The Wabash and Erie was put into the hands of trustees, who opened navigation to Terre Haute in 1849 and completed the last segment to Evansville in 1853. The cost of the entire canal was some $8.2 million.[17] Below Terre Haute, canal maintenance was poor, vandals destroyed the Birch Creek Reservoir, and only sporadic navigation was possible. The trustees struggled on until 1859, and private individuals contracted to operate the canal in sections until 1874, when the canal was sold.

Yet the traffic figures recorded at Toledo, which included the almost equally troubled Miami Extension, are larger than this checkered history might suggest. In 1851 canal traffic arriving at Toledo included 1,639,744 bushels of wheat; 242,677 barrels of flour; and 2,776,149 bushels of corn.[18] By 1851, Toledo was Ohio's leading lake port. Moreover, the Wabash and Erie and the Miami Extension offered a water route between northern Indiana and Cincinnati.[19] Although the hopes of the Indiana canal planners were not realized, Edwin Maldonado reminds us that for nine years after 1843, the Wabash and Erie Canal "was the primary carrier of both imports and exports to and from northern Indiana. . . ."[20] But the Whitewater Canal, which had wielded such political leverage, proved to be almost inoperable. Between 1847 and 1852 floods came every year but two, the last of which brought canal operations virtually to an end.[21]

Westward in Illinois, the legislative response to the demands for internal improvements came in the year following Indiana's "Mammoth Bill." In 1837 a Whig legislature, which included Abraham Lincoln, embarked on a myriad of transportation projects. But 1837 was a year of financial panic, and, of the canals, only the Illinois and Michigan Canal survived.

The Illinois River route from Lake Michigan to the Mississippi shared many of the characteristics of the Wabash trade route in Indiana or, farther north, of the Fox-Wisconsin trade route to Lake Superior. The Illinois and Michigan Canal was ninety-six miles long, from the Chicago River across the summit to the Des Plaines Valley, following that river to the rapids of the Illinois River at La Salle, below which the Illinois River could be navigated to the Mississippi. Lacking congressional assistance, Illinois chartered a company for a canal in 1825, only to repeal it in 1826. Governor Ninian Edwards helped to secure the land grant of 1827, which we have already noted was a stimulant to the Indiana canals. Nine years of controversy followed, in which railroad proponents were beaten down and sectional divisions were overcome, until, with Governor Joseph Duncan in the lead, a canal was finally authorized by the legislature in 1835.[22]

Unlike the other canals of the Old Northwest, but now more like New York's new Erie Canal, on which enlargement had just begun, the Illinois and Michigan Canal was sixty feet wide and six feet deep. Although William Gooding first surveyed the route, work did not proceed until New York's most famous engineer, Benjamin Wright, came and endorsed the plan. In spite of the Panic of 1837 and minimal sale of canal lands, money was borrowed in New York and London, and the canal was almost three fourths finished by 1842. Then the failure of the State Bank of Illinois plunged the state into a crisis over the canal similar to those which brought insolvency in Indiana in 1841, near insolvency in Ohio, and even in New York a "stop and tax" law which delayed the rebuilding of the Erie Canal. Illinois defaulted on its bonds, and the canal was deeded to trustees in 1845. As in Indiana and Ohio, sectional pressures involved demands for railroads as well as canals. After five more years of wrangling and stalemate, in which plans for a deep-cut canal were abandoned, a new tax law of 1847 allowed the completion of the canal in a year. Boats passed up the Chicago River, southwest on the canal through

Lockport, Ottawa, and Utica, to La Salle on the Illinois River, with easy passage to the Mississippi from there. With its fifteen locks and four aqueducts, the canal had cost $6.4 million.[23] Now in Congress, Abraham Lincoln announced its completion to the House of Representatives.

The Illinois and Michigan Canal was used in this form for more than a decade. In 1851 it carried to Chicago 2,878,550 bushels of corn; 78,062 bushels of wheat; 4,591,471 pounds of sugar; and 56,845,027 feet of lumber; while to the interior it carried 14,175,928 pounds of merchandise.[24] The canal did as much as the lake trade in these years to help start Chicago on its growth as the great inland lake port of the Midwest.

To the north in the Old Northwest, Wisconsin and Michigan were more lightly settled, but the expansion of internal improvements just before the Panic of 1837 prompted surveys for canals that would never be built.[25] In Wisconsin, work began in 1838 to remove the obstacles from the Fox-Wisconsin rivers portage. A congressional land grant in 1846 for this project went into effect along with Wisconsin statehood in 1848, and the Fox-Wisconsin improvement remained a state enterprise conducted under a board of public works until 1853. Since land sales could not support the enterprise, the work was pursued by successive private companies and finally by the national government, until efforts to develop a navigable through waterway were finally abandoned in 1886.[26] Only the Sault Canal on the St. Mary's River, on which work was briefly begun in 1839, added a new waterway in the upper portions of the Great Lakes.

To build the short Sault Canal at the rapids of the St. Mary's River, a canal less than a mile in length, Michigan received a land grant from Congress in 1852 after years of frustrating delay—much like the delays that had plagued the canal at the falls of the Ohio at Louisville and still prevented completion of a canal between the Fox and the Wisconsin rivers.[27] A New York company headed by Erastus Corning was awarded a contract to build the Sault Canal, with support from canal land sales, and New York engineers were engaged. In Michigan the work was directed first by Charles G. Harvey, then more effectively by John W. Brooks, and in 1853 the canal with its two deepwater locks was finished, at a cost of not quite a million dollars.[28] The state had its canal, but the company

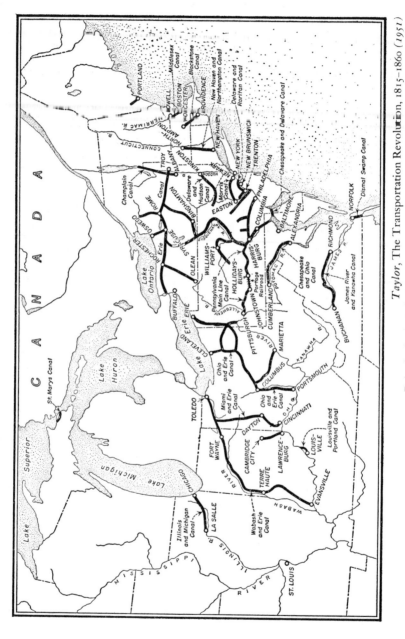

Taylor, The Transportation Revolution, 1815–1860 *(1951)*

Principal canals built by 1860

won the rich mineral lands of the land grant, which provided the basis for speculation that deeply affected the development of northern Michigan. On the canal, copper and iron from the upper peninsula were the major articles of commerce, the former reaching more than 9,000 tons and the latter swelling to 120,000 tons in 1860.[29] The Sault Canal, like the canals on the Ohio and on the Illinois River, would become obsolete and then would be rebuilt.

Dramatic as these canals of the Old Northwest were, they were western extensions of eastern waterways, especially of the Erie Canal. De Witt Clinton wrote to William Stickney of Indiana in 1817, when Stickney anticipated the Wabash and Erie Canal: "I have found a way to get into Lake Erie, and you have shown me how to get out of it. . . . You have extended my project six hundred miles."[30] But the canals of the Old Northwest were linked to the canals of Pennsylvania as well. Pennsylvania faced the decision whether to imitate New York or risk the new technology of the railroad from Philadelphia to the Ohio River.[31] The decision was made to build a canal, and the Pennsylvania Mainline Canal, with its famous incline, crossed the mountains and opened a route which Ohioans could reach with the Sandy and Beaver Canal or the Pennsylvania and Ohio. The Chesapeake and Ohio Canal stretched westward from the Potomac toward the Ohio. In New England the Middlesex Canal had been the model for the Erie Canal and was followed by the New Haven and Northampton and the Blackstone canals. On the mid-Atlantic coast were the Morris Canal, the Delaware and Raritan, and the Chesapeake and Delaware. The James River and Kanawha Canal in Virginia began a route from Richmond to the Ohio country. Still farther south were the Dismal Swamp and the Santee canals.

Moreover, Harvey H. Segal has placed the expansion of the canals of the Old Northwest in a second cycle of canal construction from 1834 to 1844, matching them with developments in national business cycles.[32] Thus the lateral canals in Ohio, the "Mammoth Bill" in Indiana, and the Illinois and Michigan Canal were part of a cycle which included the enlargement of the Erie Canal and new construction in Pennsylvania, Maryland, and Virginia. It was the crisis in the national economy in 1839 which brought default in Pennsylvania and Maryland in the East, and in Indiana and Illinois in the Old Northwest.

The canal era was a phase of the Transportation Revolution

described in a classic study by George Rogers Taylor. In this revolution the trans-Appalachian interior was opened to the East; the cost of transportation fell dramatically from more than ten cents per ton mile to as little as a cent; a canal network of 3,326 miles was built by 1840 at a cost of more than $125 million, and the way was opened for the railroad to follow.[33] These canals belong to the nationalism of the era, so frequently articulated as the Fourth of July was chosen to celebrate the beginning or the opening of a new waterway. This nationalism made canals part of an egalitarian social process, called for the strengthening of national unity, sought to mitigate sectional divisions, and celebrated the achievements of republican institutions.[34]

Strong as this nationalism may have been, too much should not be claimed for the canals as a national system. To treat the canals exclusively as a system is to overlook the localism and the self-interest they displayed. The canals of the Old Northwest were built primarily to link the Ohio and the Mississippi with the Great Lakes, and too many were anachronistic ventures designed to satisfy local competition or sectional rivalry. Communities fought to see that a canal stopped with them, or that a rival route was defeated. States adjusted canal tolls so competitively as to evade the constitutional prohibition against interstate tariffs.[35]

The issue of internal improvements was almost constantly vexed. The canals of the Old Northwest were related to nationalistic plans or dreams for a national system of roads and canals as projected by Albert Gallatin in 1806, Peter B. Porter in his report to Congress in 1810, John C. Calhoun in his Bonus Bill of 1819, the General Survey Act of 1824, and the great but unrealized internal improvements program of John Quincy Adams. One result of such plans was the national land grants to the states. However, with the advent of the administration of President Andrew Jackson, it became clear that state and sectional rivalries would prevent a broad program of national canal building and that canals would be built by states, localities, and publicly assisted private companies.[36] By the time of Jackson's presidency, the prospects for great national projects had dimmed, partly because Jackson gave them only limited support. In 1834 he spoke like the Delphic Oracle: "I am not hostile to internal improvements, and wish to see them extended to every part of the country." But, he added, "if they are not constructed in a proper manner, confined to proper objects, and conducted under an authority generally conceded to be rightful . . . a successful prosecution of them cannot reasonably be expected."[37]

Since the 1950s, historians have emphasized the role of state and local government in giving aid to these canals. The canal era was a product of the "activist state," and the role of government was recognized as necessary to give constructive stimulus to economic development.[38] In some states there was an initial distrust of private corporations for constructing canals. Such a proposal in Ohio was rejected by the legislature, though after 1837 the state turned to what has been called "mixed enterprise." In Illinois a similar proposal for private construction of the Illinois and Michigan Canal was also rejected. National aids to canals chiefly took the form of land grants to the states, and in most cases the states were the primary agents of construction. Whatever the record of state canal construction, it was public support that allowed the early nation to breach the Appalachian barrier and draw the trade of the Old Northwest to the East.

It is important to see the canals of the Old Northwest as the work of men who combined public service with private gain. Like Clinton in New York, there were redoubtable figures in the Old Northwest who made the cause of the state canals their own. Alfred Kelley was the De Witt Clinton of Ohio. He came from New York to Cleveland and later moved to Columbus. As a canal commissioner, he chose the Cuyahoga Valley route for the Ohio and Erie Canal with great integrity and political skill, and he supervised canal construction from Cleveland to Akron. As a canal fund commissioner after 1841, he developed his financial relationships with the Commercial Bank of Lake Erie, the Franklin Bank of Columbus, and the Ohio Life Insurance and Trust Company—all of which provided indispensable deposit and disbursement services for the Canal Fund Board. Kelley sold Ohio bonds in England, and in the critical year of 1842 he used his personal property to guarantee the interest on canal bonds. In the 1850s he turned to railroads, some of which followed routes he had surveyed for canals.[39]

The Ohio canals were almost a joint venture between Kelley and Micajah T. Williams of Cincinnati. Williams wrote the canal bill of 1823 and won Cincinnati support for the initial two-canal plan. He surveyed the southern part of the Ohio and Erie Canal with equal concern for engineering and politics, and he surveyed the Miami Canal. His canal experiences also led to banking, as he organized the Clinton Bank at Columbus and was president of the Ohio Life Insurance and Trust Company, which bought canal bonds and helped to finance both the Miami Extension and the Wabash and Erie Canal. His interests encompassed the Old Northwest; he was in the Louisville and Portland Canal Company, was president of the Cincinnati and Whitewater Canal Company, and he speculated in lands in Toledo, Milwaukee, and the copper country of Michigan.[40]

In Indiana a comparable figure was Samuel Hanna. A pioneer fur trader who had arrived in Fort Wayne in 1819, he led in the movement for the Wabash and Erie Canal. Like Kelley and Williams, he was both a canal commissioner doing his own surveys and a canal fund commissioner, who was associated with eastern banks and assisted in organizing the State Bank of Indiana. In 1828, five years after Kelley and Williams had gone to New York to inspect the Erie Canal, Hanna went to New York to get canal survey instruments. His land speculation around Fort Wayne and far down the Wabash Valley, his milling interests, and his leadership in Fort Wayne railroads are aspects of a life remarkably similar to that of Kelley and Williams in Ohio.[41]

Of similar distinction was John W. Brooks in Michigan. He had come from Massachusetts, where he had studied engineering with Loammi Baldwin, Jr.; he superintended railroads in New York and Michigan; and he became the man most responsible for the completion of the Sault Canal. Vice-president of the St. Mary's Falls Ship Canal Company, Brooks was a key figure in determining that the completed canal was transferred from his company to Michigan, while the mineral and pine lands of the national land grant were reserved for his company.[42] Both decisions were to have enormous significance for the development of the Old Northwest.[43]

The canal engineers were a group of almost heroic figures in the development of transportation in the Old Northwest. At a time when the science of engineering was little known in America and canal building demanded new technological precision, New Yorkers came to help build the canals of the Old Northwest. Benjamin Wright, known as the chief engineer of the Erie Canal, brought his knowledge to the Illinois and Michigan Canal in 1837. James Geddes, who discovered the line that carried the Erie Canal across western

New York, also found the crucial line across the Licking summit in Ohio. David Bates and Nathan Roberts were most responsible for the works at the western terminus of the Erie Canal. Bates helped locate the Louisville and Portland Canal, and Bates and Roberts surveyed the line of the Miami Canal. They taught Jesse B. Williams, the brother of Micajah Williams, who subsequently moved west from the Miami Canal and the Ohio and Erie Canal to become chief engineer on the Wabash and Erie Canal. Samuel S. Forrer was an Ohioan who learned his trade from Jesse Williams on the Miami Canal and then worked with him on the Miami Extension and on the Wabash and Erie. On the Sault Canal, New York engineers L. L. Nichols, John W. Clark, and William J. McAlpine came to work under the superintendence of John W. Brooks.[44]

The neat lines that show canal routes on our maps seldom reveal the problems these men confronted and the conditions under which they worked. Geddes was debilitated by his work on the Ohio canals, and disease took the life of Seymour Skiff, a New York engineer who came out to Ohio to work in 1823. After fourteen days on the job, he died of malaria and was replaced by another New Yorker, William Price. The achievements of these and other engineers are inestimable. The remarkable 1,600-foot tunnel on the Cincinnati and Whitewater Canal was one of only five such tunnels in the nation.[45] Reservoirs that covered thousands of acres were created to furnish steady supplies of canal water. The staircase of locks at Lockington, Ohio, matched the oft-pictured five-lock combine at Lockport, New York.

Such engineering triumphs were built in a time and place of labor shortage. Most familiar are the assertions and assumptions that they were accomplished with immigrant labor. Studies of the Indiana, Ohio, and Michigan canals all show reliance on Irish and German labor, with some immigrants moving from canal to canal. Maurice Cody, an Irish immigrant, came to America in 1825, worked on canals in New York, Pennsylvania, and Maryland, and then moved to Fort Wayne in 1834 to dig canals in Indiana.[46] But few examples of immigrant labor are so specific. Immigrant labor on the canals is a subject ripe for examination with the tools of the quantitative historian and new approaches to social mobility. Generalization is difficult, since contracts were local, both skilled and unskilled labor was required, and native as well as foreign immigrants came

to the Old Northwest. A study of labor on the Ohio and Erie Canal
states that "the principal source for canal labor, as may be expected,
was found in the local populace."[47] While Irish and German immigrants were added to the labor force, native New Englanders were
adding their leaven to the Western Reserve, to Cincinnati, and to
Indiana. For example, Asa Fairfield came from Kennebunk, Maine,
and built the first canal boat on the Wabash and Erie Canal.

For the states of the Old Northwest, the canal network placed
its imprint upon an age. A canal boat occupies the center of the seal
for the state of Ohio in 1860. Canal societies, county historical societies, and preservationists seek to locate and interpret the remains
of the canals and many restorations offer a glimpse of the canals as
they may have been. How precisely can the economic impact of
these canals on their era be measured or described?

Most accounts have acclaimed the Erie Canal as the only true
success of the canal era, and in a recent summary by Peter Temin
it is represented as the only one to have a significant effect on
American economic growth.[48] The canals of the Old Northwest
have attracted intensive scholarly analysis of their profitability and
social return. Roger L. Ransom concludes that the Ohio and Erie
Canal and the Miami Canal were sound investments, but the Ohio
laterals and the Miami Extension were "an unmitigated economic
loss."[49] Ransom also concluded that the Wabash and Erie Canal
was never economically viable. A recent American economic history survey by Lance E. Davis and others describes the Wabash
and Erie Canal as the least successful of all antebellum canals and
the Illinois and Michigan Canal as a "financial disaster."[50] But
Ransom has also noted that even these economic failures were part
of a canal network that for twenty-five years brought "huge reduc-
tions" in transportation costs, encouraged settlement, and opened
markets for Ohio and Indiana wheat.[51]

In the last three decades, economic historians have provided new
concepts and refined measurements to demonstrate the contribution
of canals to the rapid growth of the American economy in the first
half of the nineteenth century. They note "developmental" canals
built ahead of settled areas, as compared with "exploitative" canals
serving already established cities.[52] It is the developmental benefits
to the Old Northwest and the nation that demonstrate the contribution of canals, including agricultural expansion and the export of

agricultural surpluses, the import of eastern merchandise, and economic diversification towards manufacturing and commerce.[53] If the Erie Canal is singled out as having the greatest impact on the economic growth of the early nation, it drew much of its trade from the economic development of the Old Northwest—development stimulated by western canals.

We often find a transition in terms used to describe the canal era. From canals as a shining example of public enterprise, we move to phrases such as the "canal craze" or "the canal mania." Often this is selective: Indiana and Illinois were more profligate; Ohio was promiscuous with its Loan Law of 1836 but survived with its credit intact. Indiana built the longest canal through the least settled area, opting for the more conservative choice of the canal over the railroad. Yet George Rogers Taylor has written that "no state became more disastrously involved in the general enthusiasm for canal building than Indiana."[54] R. Carlyle Buley's comprehensive study of the Old Northwest suggests an almost universal tendency toward financial disaster in canal building.[55]

Part of the overbuilding resulted from regional rivalry, economic conditions in Harvey Segal's "second cycle" of canal building, and what Harry Scheiber has called "a variant of the egalitarian political ideology that pervaded popular thought in the 1820's and 1830's."[56] For perspective, if we note the later overbuilding in railroad construction with parallel lines and speculative financing, the canal era suffers little by comparison. Moreover, the depression in the national economy in 1837 was inevitable chiefly in hindsight. Adoption of the railroad in its limited technological development on the scale attempted by canals might have been judged greater folly than the mania for canals, and we cannot know the consequences of even a few years' delay. Though Indiana's Governor James B. Ray proposed a railroad in lieu of the Wabash and Erie Canal and a similar alternative was proposed for the Miami Extension, the canal builders could not know that the railroad would deny the more viable canals the chance either to test their capacity to recover from the depression of 1837 or to shake off the restraints of unwise extensions.

Despite its financial failures, the canal era deserves to be studied as a time when the river valley attracted settlement and commerce, when people lived in a water-connected society. The series of similar obstructions on the Wabash trade route, between the Illinois and Des Plaines rivers, between the Fox and the Wisconsin rivers, or at the rapids of the St. Mary's River, all cried out for improvement. Westerners took a successful canal technology from New York and carried it far inland. They built canals along rivers which had always been too low, too high, or too obstructed, and imposed the order and system of the canal.

The states of the Old Northwest and the companies they chartered built mile upon mile of canal, with towpath on one side and berm on the other. Locks by the hundreds were hewn out of stone and set in mortar, and then equipped with ingenious gates to control tons of water, boat, and cargo. Dozens of aqueducts carried their canals over streams, resting imposingly on their piers, adequately watertight in their wooden troughs. Canal levels were found and pitched with enough drop for a moderate current, passing over countless culverts and taking water from rivers, feeders, or reservoirs. These works were maintained by lock tenders, toll collectors, and repair crews—creating bureaucratic challenges for underdeveloped state governments. Our burgeoning canal historical societies have been reconstructing our sense of the operation of a lock, the majesty of the aqueduct, the tandem harness of horses or mules, and the distinctions among packets, line boats, and freighters.

Thousand upon thousand of passengers found travel on the new packets, at a steady five or six miles per hour, often exhilarating, often tedious, with as little agreement as to comfort as has met other means of travel. Compared to stage or wagon, canal boat travel was smooth, seemed effortless, and the close banks or forest enhanced the sense of speed. Day and night travel changed the concept of distance, and if sleeping on three-tiered bunks in the packets was warm and close, depending on the season, food on board was often reported as plentiful and excellent. Accounts of fighting and rowdiness on the canals have probably been overdrawn.[57]

Boatbuilding became a new interior industry; forwarding companies offered new enterprise; waste waters turned the wheels of new mills; warehouses and groceries lined the canals; and canal basins added hustle and bustle to isolated communities. The canals brought new settlers to the Old Northwest in its period of most rapid growth. Land grants to the states for canals, too little considered here, became objects of speculation and determined the rates and patterns of settlement.

Established urban centers such as Cincinnati, Chillicothe, Cleveland, and Toledo in Ohio competed vigorously for canals and grew with the canals they won. Each town or city served by canal is a partial measure of the canal as an instrument of growth: Akron at the Portage summit; Columbus on a feeder; Dayton as a canal terminus; Milan as an inland lakeport; Chicago as a city stimulated by a canal before it became a rail center, and in Indiana, a long line of interior towns and cities. Fort Wayne was transformed from an Indian trading center at a portage place into a canal town. Fort Wayne, Huntington, Wabash, Peru, Lafayette, Logansport, Delphi, Covington, and Attica grew with the canal and continued to develop with the railroad. Lagro, Lewisburg, Georgetown, Carrollton, Americus, Lockport, and Pittsburg flourished only so long as the canal sustained them.[58]

In the canal era an enterprising generation made the canals central to their lives. They used their new state governments to provide a canal network that often served them well until depression struck or until the railroad passed it by. The long lines of the canals now drawn on our maps are only the skeletal remains of a once vital dimension in the growth of the Old Northwest.

NOTES

1. Monographs for canals in the states of the Old Northwest include Harry N. Scheiber, *Ohio Canal Era: A Case Study of Government and the Economy, 1820–1861* (Athens: Ohio University Press, 1969); Paul Fatout, *Indiana Canals* (West Lafayette, Ind.: Purdue University Studies, 1972); John H. Krenkel, *Illinois Internal Improvements, 1818–1848* (Cedar Rapids, Iowa: Torch Press, 1958); John N. Dickinson, *To Build a Canal: Sault Ste. Marie, 1853–1854 and After* (Columbus: Miami-Ohio State University Press, 1981); and Samuel Mermin, *The Fox-Wisconsin Rivers Improvement: An Historical Study in Legal Institutions and Political Economy* (Madison: University Extension, Law Department, University of Wisconsin, 1968). For the canal era as a whole the best survey is George Rogers Taylor, *The Transportation Revolution, 1815–1860* (New York: Rinehart & Co., 1951). The Old Northwest in this period is given comprehensive study in R. Carlyle Buley, *The Old Northwest: Pioneer Period, 1815–1840* (2 volumes. Indianapolis: Indiana Historical Society, 1950).

2. Fatout, *Indiana Canals*, pp. 6, 17. The short length and great service of this canal invites comparison with the last major canal in the canal era in the Old Northwest, the Sault Canal in upper Michigan. See Dickinson, *Sault Ste. Marie*, p. 37; Paul B. Trescott, "The Louisville and Portland Canal Com-

pany, 1825–1874," in *Mississippi Valley Historical Review*, XLIV (1957–1958), 686–708; Erik F. Haites, James Mak, and Gary M. Walton, *Western River Transportation: The Era of Internal Development, 1810–1860* (Baltimore: Johns Hopkins University Press, 1975), pp. 91–94.

3. Scheiber, *Ohio Canal Era*, pp. 15–30; Harry N. Scheiber, "The Ohio Canal Movement, 1820–1825," in *Ohio Historical Quarterly*, LXIX (1960), 231–56; Harry N. Scheiber, "Urban Rivalry and Internal Improvements in the Old Northwest, 1820–1860," in *Ohio History*, LXXI (1962), 228–32. Most studies of the Ohio canals draw upon C. P. McClelland and C. C. Huntington, *History of the Ohio Canals: Their Construction, Use and Partial Abandonment* (Columbus: Ohio State Archaeological and Historical Society, 1905).

4. Harry N. Scheiber, "Public Canal Finance and State Banking in Ohio, 1827–1837," in *Indiana Magazine of History*, LXV (1969), 129.

5. Scheiber, *Ohio Canal Era*, p. 53.

6. *Ibid.*, pp. 11, 130–33. For a recent examination of this policy see Harry N. Scheiber, "The Pennsylvania & Ohio Canal: Transport Innovation, Mixed Enterprise, and Urban Commercial Rivalry, 1825–1861," in *The Old Northwest*, VI (1980), 105–35.

7. The Miami Extension Canal was built to the dimensions of fifty feet by five feet and cost almost $7 million. It was aided by a land grant of 1,200,000 acres, which included Ohio's part of the Wabash and Erie Canal grant and an additional "floating grant" of 500,000 acres, from which Ohio received $2,257,487. John Bell Rae, "Federal Land Grants in Aid of Canals," in *Journal of Economic History*, IV (1944), 167–77, and Harry N. Scheiber, "Land Reform, Speculation, and Governmental Failure: The Administration of Ohio's State Canal Lands, 1836–60," in *Prologue: The Journal of the National Archives*, VII (1975), 85–98.

8. Scheiber, *Ohio Canal Era*, p. 112.

9. *Ibid.*, pp. 193–95, 198–200, 238.

10. *Ibid.*, p. 202. See also Richard T. Farrell, "Internal-Improvement Projects in Southwestern Ohio, 1815–1834," in *Ohio History*, LXXX (1971), 4–23.

11. Net yearly earnings averaged $221,000 in the period 1835–1840; $295,000 for 1841–1845; and $395,000 for 1846–1850. These figures reflected a steady lowering of tolls. Scheiber, *Ohio Canal Era*, pp. 237, 259–63, 300, 380–86.

12. Congress granted 527,271.24 acres, 5 miles wide for 160 miles from the Tippecanoe River to the Auglaize River in Ohio. Rae, "Federal Land Grants in Aid of Canals," in *Journal of Economic History*, IV, 170; Fatout, *Indiana Canals*, p. 39; Elbert J. Benton, *The Wabash Trade Route in the Development of the Old Northwest* (Johns Hopkins University *Studies in History and Political Science*, Series XXI, Nos. 1–2, Baltimore, 1903), p. 45. John Tipton also helped to secure Indian reserve lands along the canal route. Tipton, Samuel Hanna, Hugh Hanna, David Burr, Chauncey Carter, Hugh B. McKeen, and Joseph Holman all speculated in Indian reserves and canal lands. Edwin Maldonado, "Urban Growth during the Canal Era: The Case of

Indiana," in *Indiana Social Studies Quarterly*, XXXI, No. 3 (1978–1979), pp. 22–23. For an early study of the Indiana canals see Logan Esarey, *Internal Improvements in Early Indiana* (Indiana Historical Society *Publications*, V, Indianapolis, 1912).

13. R. Carlyle Buley referred to the Whitewater Canal as the "key to the whole logrolling process. . . ." Buley, *The Old Northwest*, II, 261.

14. See Julius Rubin, *Canal or Railroad? Imitation and Innovation in the Response to the Erie Canal in Philadelphia, Baltimore, and Boston* (American Philosophical Society, *Transactions*, LI, Pt. 7, Philadelphia, 1961).

15. Fatout, *Indiana Canals*, pp. 50, 78–81; Rae, "Federal Land Grants in Aid of Canals," in *Journal of Economic History*, IV, 173.

16. With the completion of the Cincinnati and Whitewater Canal, a route was open to Cincinnati which became the major outlet for the trade of the Whitewater Valley. The Hagerstown Canal Company extended the Whitewater Canal north to Hagerstown. See articles by Jane Lucy in *The Hagerstown Exponent*, March 25, April 1, 8, 15, 1981.

17. Esarey, *Internal Improvements in Indiana*, p. 155.

18. Benton, *The Wabash Trade Route*, p. 102.

19. Particularly poignant is the use of this canal route in 1846, when 325 Indians boarded canal boats at Fort Wayne to take the Wabash and Erie Canal to Defiance, the Miami Extension Canal to Dayton, and the Miami Canal to Cincinnati, in their removal from their Wabash lands to Kansas. Charles R. Poinsatte, *Fort Wayne during the Canal Era, 1828–1855 (Indiana Historical Collections*, XLVI, Indianapolis: Indiana Historical Bureau, 1969), p. 102.

20. Maldonado also concludes that "as an outlet for produce the canal did the job its boosters had predicted." Maldonado, "Urban Growth during the Canal Era," in *Indiana Social Studies Quarterly*, XXXI, No. 3, pp. 21, 28. More typical is the early judgment of Logan Esarey: "A magnificent land grant by the federal government had been squandered." Esarey, *Internal Improvements in Early Indiana*, p. 155. For more recent conclusions that the Wabash and Erie Canal was an economic failure see below, note 50.

21. Paul Fatout estimated that annual income never exceeded $30,000. Fatout, *Indiana Canals*, p. 152.

22. James William Putnam, *The Illinois and Michigan Canal: A Study in Economic History* (Chicago Historical Society *Collections*, X, Chicago: University of Chicago Press, 1918), p. 29.

23. Krenkel, *Illinois Internal Improvements*, p. 195.

24. Putnam, *The Illinois and Michigan Canal*, p. 102. In 1850 the canal carried 22,614 passengers from Chicago to La Salle and 17,000 from La Salle to Chicago. John M. Lamb, "Early Days on the Illinois & Michigan Canal," in *Chicago History*, new series, III (1974–1975), 174.

25. In Michigan construction began on a Mount Clemens-Kalamazoo Canal in 1837, and a canal was authorized from the Saginaw River to the Maple River. In Wisconsin a company was chartered for a canal from Milwaukee to the Rock River, with a branch to the Fox River. Congress granted

138,996 acres for this canal in 1838. Rae, "Federal Land Grants in Aid of Canals," in *Journal of Economic History*, IV, 170; Buley, *The Old Northwest*, II, 265, 267, 299; Dickinson, *Sault Ste. Marie*, pp. 20–21.

26. See Mermin, *The Fox-Wisconsin Rivers Improvement*.

27. Congress gave a land grant for the Sault Ste. Marie Canal of 750,000 acres. Rae, "Federal Land Grants in Aid of Canals," in *Journal of Economic History*, IV, 175; Dickinson, *Sault Ste. Marie*, pp. 26–30; Irene D. Neu, "The Building of the Sault Canal, 1852–1855," in *Mississippi Valley Historical Review*, XL, (1953), 28; Irene D. Neu, "The Mineral Lands of the St. Mary's Falls Ship Canal Company," in David M. Ellis (ed.), *The Frontier in American Development: Essays in Honor of Paul Wallace Gates* (Ithaca, N.Y.: Cornell University Press, 1969), pp. 162ff.

28. Dickinson, *Sault Ste. Marie*, p. 126.

29. *Ibid.*, p. 130.

30. Benton, *The Wabash Trade Route*, p. 94.

31. See Julius Rubin, "An Imitative Public Improvement: The Pennsylvania Mainline," in Carter Goodrich (ed.), *Canals and American Economic Development* (New York: Columbia University Press, 1961), pp. 67–114.

32. Harvey H. Segal, "Cycles of Canal Construction," in Goodrich (ed.), *Canals and American Economic Development*, pp. 189–203.

33. Taylor, *The Transportation Revolution*, chap. 3. On the Ohio and Erie Canal the ton-mile cost was 1 cent; on the Illinois and Michigan Canal it was 1.4 cents.

34. Paul C. Nagel, *One Nation Indivisible: The Union in American Thought, 1776–1861* (New York: Oxford University Press, 1964), p. 91; Albert H. Kohlmeier, *The Old Northwest as the Keystone of the Arch of American Federal Union* (Bloomington, Ind.: Principia Press, 1938), pp. 127–28, 244–47; Ronald E. Shaw, *Erie Water West: A History of the Erie Canal, 1792–1854* (Lexington: University of Kentucky Press, 1966), chap. 19; Scheiber, *Ohio Canal Era*, pp. 89–91; Ralph D. Gray, *The National Waterway: A History of the Chesapeake and Delaware Canal, 1769–1965* (Urbana: University of Illinois Press, 1967), p. 42.

35. Harry N. Scheiber, "The Rate-Making Power of the State in the Canal Era: A Case Study," in *Political Science Quarterly*, LXXVII (1962), 413; Scheiber, *Ohio Canal Era*, chap. 10; Scheiber, "The Pennsylvania & Ohio Canal," in *The Old Northwest*, VI, 122–26.

36. Carter Goodrich, *Government Promotion of American Canals and Railroads, 1800–1890* (New York: Columbia University Press, 1960), pp. 41–48.

37. James D. Richardson (comp.), *A Compilation of the Messages and Papers of the Presidents, 1789–1897* (Washington, D.C.: Government Printing Office, 1896), III, 122–23. Nor were political parties consistent in their attitudes toward internal improvements. In Indiana, Whigs advocated allowing indebtedness for canal construction, while the Democrats were more opposed. In Illinois, an opposite alignment emerged. In Ohio, Alfred Kelley was a Whig and Micajah Williams was a Democrat, yet both worked ardently

for the Ohio canals, though after 1836 canal offices in Ohio increasingly reflected party politics and patronage. In New York, as elsewhere, the Hunker or more conservative wing of the Democratic party was more willing to support indebtedness for internal improvements, while the Locofoco or more radical wing was more opposed.

38. By 1860, approximately 70 percent of the total investment in canals was public investment. Segal, "Cycles of Canal Construction," in Goodrich (ed.), *Canals and American Development*, pp. 172, 215. Carter Goodrich concludes that this "impetus to economic development" was the result of "using the resources of government to provide the improvements which private enterprise could not yet supply." Goodrich (ed.), *Canals and Economic Development*, p. 255.

39. Kelley wrote the Ohio state bank law of 1845 and then devised a new tax policy for the state. Harry N. Scheiber, "Alfred Kelley and the Ohio Business Elite, 1822–1859," in *Ohio History*, LXXXVII (1978), 386–87.

40. See Harry N. Scheiber, "Entrepreneurship and Western Development: The Case of Micajah T. Williams," in *Business History Review*, XXXVII (1963), 345–68.

41. Poinsatte, *Fort Wayne*, pp. 86, 112–13; Fatout, *Indiana Canals*, p. 41; Benton, *The Wabash Trade Route*, pp. 90–91; see Paul W. Wehr, "Samuel Hanna: Fur Trader to Railroad Magnate" (Ph.D. dissertation, Ball State University, 1968).

42. Dickinson, *Sault Ste. Marie*, pp. 113–20.

43. Neu, "The Mineral Lands," in Ellis (ed.), *The Frontier in American Development*, pp. 175–91; Dickinson, *Sault Ste. Marie*, chaps. 11–12.

44. For accounts of the work of these engineers see Shaw, *Erie Water West*; Krenkel, *Illinois Internal Improvements*; Fatout, *Indiana Canals*; Scheiber, *Ohio Canal Era*; Scheiber, "Micajah T. Williams," in *Business History Review*, XXXVII; and Lamb, "Early Days on the Illinois & Michigan Canal," in *Chicago History*, III.

45. Two tunnels were built on the Pennsylvania mainline, and one each was built on the Schuylkill and on the Union canals.

46. Poinsatte, *Fort Wayne*, p. 65.

47. Earnest M. Teagarden, "Builders of the Ohio Canal, 1825–1832," in *Inland Seas*, XIX (1963), 95. Teagarden also notes on page 96 that inmates from the Ohio State Penitentiary were employed on the Columbus feeder.

48. Peter Temin, *Causal Factors in American Economic Growth in the Nineteenth Century* (London: Macmillan Press, 1975), p. 38.

49. Roger L. Ransom, "Public Canal Investment and the Opening of the Old Northwest," in David C. Klingaman and Richard K. Vedder (eds.), *Essays in Nineteenth Century Economic History: The Old Northwest* (Athens: Ohio University Press, 1975), pp. 254–61.

50. Lance E. Davis *et al.*, *American Economic Growth: An Economist's History of the United States* (New York: Harper & Row, 1972), pp. 480–81.

51. Ransom, "Public Canal Investment," in Klingaman and Vedder (eds.), *Essays in Nineteenth Century Economic History*, pp. 263–64. For other

studies of the Ohio canals see Roger L. Ransom, "Canals and Development: A Discussion of the Issues," in *American Economic Review*, LIV (1964), 365–76; Roger L. Ransom, "Interregional Canals and Economic Specialization in the Ante-Bellum United States," in *Explorations in Entrepreneurial History*, 2d series, V (1967–1968), 12–35; Roger L. Ransom, "Social Returns from Public Transport Investment: A Case Study of the Ohio Canal," in *Journal of Political Economy*, LXXVIII (1970), 1041–60; and Roger L. Ransom, "Government Investment in Canals: A Study of the Ohio Canal, 1825–1860" (Ph.D. dissertation, University of Washington, Seattle, 1963).

52. Harvey H. Segal, "Canals and Economic Development," in Goodrich (ed.), *Canals and American Development*, chap. 5. For developmental canals, "By lowering transport costs they hastened the progress of regional specialization, raised regional output, and were conducive to urban development" (p. 225).

53. Thus Harvey H. Segal concludes that for the Wabash and Erie Canal "if we deduct the $2 million invested on the line between Terre Haute and Evansville and consider only the northeastern portion of the canal, it is probable that the benefit conferred was equivalent to the cost." *Ibid.*, p. 245. For other studies describing the economic impact of the western canals see Albert Niemi, Jr., "A Further Look at Interregional Canals and Economic Specialization: 1820–1840," in *Explorations in Entrepreneurial History*, 2d series, VII (1969–1970), 499–520; Scheiber, *Ohio Canal Era*, chaps. 8–10; and Davis *et al.*, *American Economic Growth*, chap. 13.

54. Taylor, *The Transportation Revolution*, p. 47.

55. Buley, *The Old Northwest*, II, chap. 12.

56. Scheiber, *Ohio Canal Era*, p. 89.

57. See Shaw, *Erie Water West*, chap. 12.

58. Benton, *The Wabash Trade Route*, pp. 101–102.

The Canal Era in Indiana

RALPH D. GRAY

The canal era dawned slowly over the broad expanse of still heavily wooded land that was the Hoosier state during the 1820s and early 1830s. Other states were already feverishly involved in various internal improvements by this time. New York had completed its monumental Erie Canal in 1825 and only ten years later, because of the press of traffic, had undertaken a major enlargement program. Pennsylvania had begun extensive canal and railroad building projects, also in the 1820s, and most other states up and down the Atlantic coast were similarly involved. In the West, beyond the Appalachians, Ohio had set the pace, embarking as early as 1825 upon an extensive public works program which included not one but two Lake Erie-to-Ohio River canals.[1] But if Indiana was slow to catch the internal improvements fever, she contracted an unusually severe case of it in the mid-1830s. In December, 1834, when Governor Noah Noble addressed the Indiana General Assembly of 1834–1835, he declared that "no good reason can be assigned why we should longer hesitate to follow the successful examples of other States." Indiana should, he continued, "borrow [the] money at a fair rate of interest," devote it to "some well selected objects of paramount public utility," and thereby "enrich both" the government of the state and its people.[2]

An immediate legislative response to the governor's proposal was delayed by disagreements over specific projects and routes, but the following year, amid near universal popular applause and support from both sides of the aisle in the new Statehouse, a bill providing for "a general system of internal improvements" was adopted. Often

Ralph D. Gray is Professor of History in Indiana University, Indianapolis.

referred to as the Mammoth Internal Improvement program, the act of 1836 committed the state to eight turnpike, canal, and railroad projects estimated to cost well in excess of $10 million.[3] Quite clearly the improvement fever had reached Indiana, resulting in a major transformation of the state—its economy, its political orientation, and its societal and cultural dimensions. In the pages that follow, it will be my purpose to examine the canal components of the general system of 1836, especially, of course, the Wabash and Erie Canal; to re-examine the critical decisions regarding this canal—particularly several during the 1840s, including the so-called Butler bills of 1846 and 1847, which led to completion of the canal from the Ohio state line to Terre Haute and its extension southward all the way to Evansville; to review what has been written about the impact of canals upon Indiana; and to assess briefly what research still needs to be done.[4] In part this involves a consideration of this question: why was Indiana apparently so backward, or so foolish and shortsighted, as to ignore the railroad alternative? At a time when the canal age was on the downward slope, when the age of the iron horse and the T-rail was well under way, why did Indiana seem to look to the past rather than to the future? Is it not possible, however, that the *state's* decision (not necessarily the canal bondholders' decision) in 1846 and 1847 was the proper one, that given the historical and economic conditions at the time the legislators, in fact, acted wisely? We will return to this point after first examining some aspects of the more familiar story of Indiana's earlier experiences in canal building.

A canal age in Indiana had threatened to begin early in the nineteenth century when, on August 24, 1805, the first territorial legislature issued a charter to the Indiana Canal Company, its ostensible purpose being to construct a passage around the falls in the Ohio River near present-day Jeffersonville. However, as John Badollet remarked afterwards to Albert Gallatin, "that undertaking . . . was in my humble opinion the basis on which a plan of gigantic Speculation was intended to rest,"[5] and subsequent developments confirmed this judgment. The canal company's sponsors, among them the redoubtable Aaron Burr, were more interested in their authority to issue paper money and establish a bank than in digging a navigation channel, and several writers have concluded that this venture was intended to help finance the so-called Burr Conspiracy.[6] This association, of course, did not invalidate the significance of the canal project itself, and subsequent attempts to build a much-needed Ohio Falls Canal were made in 1817–1819, and again in the early 1820s, but they proved futile. The first canal efforts in Indiana ended, in Paul Fatout's words, "after much sound and fury signifying nothing capable of floating a boat."[7] In the meantime, Kentucky was bestirring herself and making plans to build the short bypass waterway on her side of the river. Aided by a sizable federal stock subscription granted in 1826, Kentucky, to the continuing good fortune of its major Ohio River port, completed the Louisville and Portland Canal in 1829.[8]

By the time Kentucky was putting the finishing touches upon this short and profitable canal, Indiana was becoming deeply involved with its own major improvement project, a Lake Erie–Wabash River connection, and with several other canal, as well as railroad, projections. The first and obvious waterway project was, of course, along the historic "Wabash trade route," obstructed only in the Fort Wayne area by the necessity for a portage between the Maumee and the Little Wabash rivers. The importance of this route, used by early French explorers of the Mississippi Valley, was also recognized in the Ordinance of 1787, which declared the waterways and necessary portages between the St. Lawrence and Mississippi rivers to be "common highways, and forever free," and in the writings of George Washington, who dreamed of connecting the Ohio River with the eastern seaboard not only via an extended "Potowmack" canal but also by way of a St. Lawrence—Lake Erie route.[9]

An early definite prediction of the Wabash and Erie Canal was made in 1816 by Robert B. McAfee in his *History of the Late War in the Western Country*, where he pointed to the short portage—only seven or eight miles—between the head of navigation on the Maumee to the nearest navigable branch of the Wabash. "A canal at some future day," he confidently asserted, "will unite these rivers."[10] Three years later a government surveyor, James Riley, ran a line of levels over the portage and concluded that a canal there was not only practicable but destined for greatness. Indiana's first governor, Jonathan Jennings, although a resident of distant Clark County on the Ohio, had already endorsed the concept of a state-sponsored system of roads and canals, including the Maumee-Wabash connection. Such talk excited the admiration of others, including De Witt

Clinton, famed for his promotion of the Erie Canal in New York. He exclaimed to a supporter of the Indiana canal in 1818: "I have found the way to get into Lake Erie and you have shown me how to get out of it. . . . You have extended my project six hundred miles."[11]

It is not appropriate here to review the two-decade-long congressional struggle for federal aid to internal improvements and the onset of the first wave of canal construction in America, beyond making the point that the 1820s witnessed not only considerable canal-building activity but also the initiation of federal assistance to private and state works.[12] Previous appeals usually had resulted in little more than appropriations for additional surveys, culminating in the General Survey Act of 1824, but beginning in 1825 with a $300,000 subscription to the stock of the privately owned Chesapeake and Delaware Canal Company, and in 1827 with land grants to Indiana and Illinois for canals, a new policy was adopted. Indiana Senator William Hendricks, also from southern Indiana but a longstanding advocate of the northern Wabash canal both as governor and senator, was instrumental in getting the land grant policy established.[13] The more extensive railroad land grants beginning in 1850 were the culmination of this policy. Although canal land grants totaled less than 5 million acres compared to approximately 130 million acres received by the railroads, their influence and significance were great.[14] The 1827 canal grants initiated, among other things, the alternate section pattern of such grants; they also represented the first tangible assets of improvement projects and as such served to loosen the purse strings of otherwise hesitant investors.

The land grant to Indiana, consisting of five sections (that is, 5 square miles, or 3,200 acres) of land for each mile of canal located on both sides of the right-of-way in an alternating or checkerboard pattern, was signed into law on March 2, 1827. Among the stipulations of the grant was a requirement to begin construction within five years, and to complete construction within twenty years.[15] Indiana promptly accepted the grant, thereby entering into a moral and legal commitment to build the canal. In fact, the acceptance of this land grant in 1828, and of subsequent grants for extensions of the Wabash and Erie Canal below Lafayette, proved to be the primary determinant of the future, often blighted, history of the canal. The key decisions in that history, as intimated earlier, appear to be those related to the land received from the federal government, approximately 1,500,000 acres.

At the time of the first grant, there was general enthusiasm for a Wabash and Erie canal, even if it was located in remote northeastern Indiana still largely inhabited by various Indian peoples. Citizens in the more populous southeastern and lower Wabash River valley recognized that the first improvement project would be of little direct value to them. Still, secure in the belief that the Wabash and Erie was merely the first step in a statewide plan for internal improvements, these persons were content to bide their time and watch the first desultory steps being taken to construct the northeastern canal. To supervise the work, the Indiana legislature had appointed a three-man canal commission and empowered it to hire engineers and surveyors, to lay out the route, and to establish a construction fund through the sale of canal lands. An immediate obstacle was encountered when it was learned that, in order to join navigable points, part of the canal must lie in Ohio. At a conference in Cincinnati between agents of the two states, however, an agreement was reached whereby Ohio would build that section of the canal within her borders in return for a proportional amount of Indiana's land grant. Again, the Indiana legislature promptly accepted the agreement, but Ohio did not do so for several years. Having just undertaken two canals to link Lake Erie with the Ohio River, Ohio did not relish giving material aid to a potential rival. Not until 1834 was the agreement accepted, and not until 1843 did Ohio complete her eighty-eight-mile portion of the canal.[16]

Other obstacles were encountered in some minor details of organization, but a major delay occurred while, in a belated second guess, the relative merits of canals and railroads were argued. Governor James B. Ray, one of the more interesting and colorful occupants of that office, had touched off the discussion in December, 1827, in his annual message to the legislature. "Railways," the governor contended, "are rapidly bearing away the palm of usefulness . . . from all other commercial facilities." They could be constructed at about half the cost of a canal, carry as much freight "with *double* the velocity," and operate in all seasons. He denied that his remarks were a recommendation of railways over canals and insisted that he simply intended to make sure that the legislature considered all the options available at the time. And he promised

that if the legislators, after due deliberation, still preferred a canal,
"as is most generally and reasonably supposed you will, I will cheer-
fully devote a portion of my time and services, in co-operation with
you, for the furtherance of this project, which has long since had
my approbation."[17]

As Governor Ray knew, waterways men in the legislature, including the "Wabash Band" in southwestern Indiana, outnumbered
the railroad men by a sizable margin, and the senate committee
which studied this portion of the governor's message responded
quickly and unequivocally. "Every consideration of usefulness,
practicability, durability, and economy," the committee concluded,
"point to Canals, and render it obviously inexpedient to waste time
upon the subject of railways."[18] At that time, of course, no railroads
were in operation in the United States, whereas the Erie Canal in
New York was still seen as an unmixed blessing to the people. Canals,
moreover, were considered to be a more democratic mode of transport than railways, since anyone could build a boat and put it into
a canal at any place, but only specially built cars, to be moved only
by the railroad company itself, were allowed on the rival system.
An "Indiana Farmer" contributed to this debate by stating that
"railroads decay, . . . whereas canals become more permanent with
time, also more profitable." Probably the most telling point in this
debate, however, was the contention that most of the supplies needed
for building and operating railroads—the track, the cars, the locomotives—would have to be imported, but the items needed for building canals—chiefly timber and stone, plus massive amounts of labor
—were available locally and would profit the citizens of Indiana,
not others.[19]

At no time, in fact, was any serious consideration given to
substituting a railroad for any portion of the Wabash and Erie Canal,
not even in 1847 when the decision was made to extend the canal
153 miles from Terre Haute to Evansville. Most canal advocates, at
least until well into the 1850s, believed in the inherent superiority of
canals to railroads, and unswervingly supported the Wabash and
Erie and related projects. While they did not object to the plans of
railroad proponents—some fifteen railroad companies were chartered in Indiana between 1832 and 1845—and welcomed all sorts of
improvements for the state, still, as a newspaper correspondent stated

in 1834, "Where water can be had to feed a Canal, [no one] should suffer himself to be misled by the rail road project. . . ."[20]

Construction of the Wabash and Erie Canal began, with appropriate ceremony, at Fort Wayne on February 22, 1832. According to the terms of the land grant act, construction had to begin by March 2, 1832, so the state met its deadline with nine days to spare. Soon the first thirty-two miles of the line between Fort Wayne and Huntington were under contract, and within two years over one thousand men, chiefly Irish laborers, were at work with pick and shovel, cart and team. Jesse L. Williams, a youthful veteran of the Miami and Erie Canal in Ohio, was chief engineer, beginning an association which lasted throughout the entire life of the Wabash and Erie.[21] Despite occasional labor problems, including a series of "Irish wars," the canal was opened from Fort Wayne to Huntington on July 4, 1835; again there was an appropriate celebration of the joyful event in Fort Wayne, and general enthusiasm for internal improvements all over the state rose perceptibly. Few anti-improvement candidates for the state legislature stood a chance of election, and the broad internal improvements sentiment across the land in the prosperous boom years of 1835 and 1836 was soon translated into legislation. In Indiana the 1835–1836 General Assembly was designated the "General System" legislature by one editor at the start of its session,[22] and it eventually responded with the previously mentioned act for a "general system of internal improvements."

By its terms the Wabash and Erie Canal was to be extended and completed to Terre Haute, some seventy-five miles below Lafayette, and two other canals, linked to one another and to the Wabash and Erie, were to be built, one in the central and southwestern part of the state, one in the southeastern area. Railroads and turnpikes were to serve other portions of Indiana.[23] This so-called Mammoth Internal Improvement act had enjoyed firm bipartisan support, and it was almost universally hailed within as well as without the state. It cannot be said that Indiana adopted its ambitious but ultimately disastrous program without due deliberation or that it was an unpopular measure. Calvin Fletcher, an Indianapolis attorney and businessman not given normally to overstatement, believed that "this grand project will exalt Indiana among the nations of the earth."[24]

The canal portions of this "system," in addition to providing for the Wabash and Erie extension, authorized the Whitewater Canal between Cambridge City on the National Road and Lawrenceburg on the Ohio River, via Connersville, Laurel, Metamora, and Brookville, and further authorized the Central Canal, to extend from a point to be determined along the Wabash and Erie near Peru all the way south to the Ohio River at Evansville via Indianapolis, Worthington, and Petersburg. Extensions linking both the Whitewater and Wabash and Erie canals with the long Central Canal, the latter project being known as the Cross-cut Canal from Terre Haute to Worthington, were also laid out, but of these projects only the Whitewater was completed as planned. Both the Cross-cut and the southern sections of the Central Canal were incorporated later into an expanded version of the Wabash and Erie line in 1847, thereby linking Terre Haute and Evansville by water just shortly before a railroad between the two cities was completed.

The Whitewater Canal had been the favorite project of the populous southeastern counties of the state for years, and a route down the steep valley had long since been laid out. There was a drop of almost five hundred feet along the seventy-six-mile line, requiring fifty-six locks and several dams and aqueducts in order to tame the rampaging waters. Work commenced immediately following the legislative authorization, and some thirty miles up from Lawrenceburg were completed before all internal improvement construction was suspended by the state in 1839. Three years later, responding to a desperate state offer, a private company acquired the canal property and pushed it to completion by 1846. The canal, in operation for approximately twenty years, was particularly susceptible to flood damage because of the steep hills and rugged terrain through which it passed and on account of some bad engineering decisions, but it proved useful to the residents of the Whitewater Valley for a generation. In 1865 operations on the canal ceased, and a railroad using the towpath for its track bed was completed through the valley in 1867.[25]

Although the short-lived Whitewater Canal was an economic asset to its area, the same cannot be said of the Central Canal. Only short segments in Marion and Morgan counties were completed, and the little stretch of canal which has been preserved in Indianapolis stands today as a reminder of the overzealousness of the internal improvement architects of 1836. More than $880,000 was expended in constructing the waterway, but when it was sold by the state at auction in 1859, it brought in only $2,425. Now a scenic property of the Indianapolis Water Company and popular with joggers and hikers, the Central Canal represents the impotence and bad credit of the state after the collapse of its economy in 1839.[26]

There is no need here to repeat details of the familiar story of the downfall of the general system of 1836. Fraud and mismanagement were partly responsible; also to blame were outside events, such as the panic and depression of the late 1830s and early 1840s and the failure of major state creditors, particularly the Morris Canal and Banking Company. The attempt to construct all the projects in the system simultaneously was undoubtedly the final blow. The strategy resulted in ruinous labor costs, so that no project was completed before all work was halted in 1839.[27] Soon the state was unable to pay even the interest on its bonded debt, much less to settle with its surveyors, contractors, and engineers. When additional bonds were offered in 1841 to raise funds for the overdue interest payments, no market for them could be found. The state was forced to announce its inability to service its debt any longer, but the legislature nobly asserted its intentions to resume payments on interest and principal as soon as possible. It also authorized the transfer of the abandoned projects to private companies, which could complete the unfinished portions and then operate those sections. Only the Wabash and Erie Canal was retained to be completed by the state, because it was believed the federal land grant carried this obligation.[28]

Consequently, the state pushed ahead with the canal, at least twice resorting to canal scrip (known as "White Dog" and "Blue Dog" from the color of paper used) rather than cash to pay its workmen.[29] By 1841 the canal was sufficiently complete to permit navigation between Fort Wayne and Lafayette, and plans were under way to begin construction below Lafayette all the way to Terre Haute. A ray of hope had come when Congress confirmed a land grant, under the terms of the 1827 act, for the entire distance to Terre Haute. This amounted to an additional grant of some 260,000 acres, which it was estimated would and, in fact, did sell for an average of more than $4 an acre, bringing to the project over $1 million.[30] A second major boost came in 1843, when Ohio finally opened the section between the Indiana–Ohio state line and the junction of the Wabash and Erie–Miami and Erie canals near Defiance. The way was now open for navigation from Lafayette to Toledo and points eastward. The canal boat *Albert S. White*, appropriately named for a prominent Whig politician in the state, completed the passage through to Toledo on May 8. Two months later, on July 4, 1843, Fort Wayne hosted its most lavish canal celebration ever. Paul Fatout's description of the event is memorable.

> ... A sunrise salute of twenty-six guns initiated an artillery barrage that boomed all morning. Double tiers of boats decorated with flags lined the wharf the length of the town, from Lafayette Street to Harrison, and hospitable residents opened their doors to all comers, dispensing good cheer by collation, by decanter, and jug. The Toledo Guards came to town, a band from Defiance, Governor Ethan Allen Brown of Ohio, farmers and villagers from miles around. Prominent gentlemen, unable to attend, sent regrets: Martin Van Buren, Winfield Scott, Henry Clay, Daniel Webster. General Lewis Cass, orator of the day, sailed in from Toledo on the packet *Ohio*, reception committee and crowd at dockside to welcome the distinguished guest with proper acclaim. Unfortunately the aging general, attempting to step casually ashore while acknowledging plaudits, missed his footing and fell into the canal.
>
> The ducking did not take the starch out of his rhetoric. After a monster parade of citizens notable and venerable, three bands, Miami Indians and others, and a great free barbecue, General Cass, last of five speakers, delivered a masterly oration reported in seven newspaper columns of fine print.[31]

This was followed by thirteen regular and several volunteer toasts, and then more "martial pomp and . . . cheers, stirring music, and the window-rattling roar of gunfire."[32] Equally impressive, a brisk trade on the canal commenced, and land sales along the entire line of the canal were numerous. The discouraging side of the picture, however, was the reality of a $13.9 million state debt, which, since no interest was being paid, was increasing at the disheartening rate of $.5 million a year.

At this point something occurred which no student of the canal's history has yet examined in sufficient detail. The third and largest canal land grant was made to the state by the federal government.[33]

This grant was in response to an 1843 legislative petition for the land, itself a response to desperate waterways men in the southwestern pocket of the state seeking some of the improvement benefits for themselves and their farm products.[34] What is noteworthy here is that the grant included not only the alternate sections along the canal line itself, but all of the unsold land in the Vincennes Land District, land that had been on the market since the Vincennes land office had opened in 1804. Together this grant exceeded 766,000 acres of land, valued from $2 million to $3 million. For those who wonder at the state's, and the bondholders', decision to complete the Wabash and Erie Canal from Terre Haute to Evansville, a large part of the answer can be found right here. Indeed, as Paul Fatout remarks but does not develop the point, "The donation guaranteed a canal [to Evansville]."[35]

The guarantee was conditional, of course, upon Indiana's accepting both the grant and the implied obligation, and this acceptance was by no means automatic. Various canal meetings were held in the lower Wabash Valley during 1845 to promote completion of the canal by accepting the grant and getting on with the work. Significantly, Charles Butler of New York attended the meeting at Terre Haute in May and at Evansville in November. Butler is best known as the extraordinarily effective lobbyist for the foreign creditors of the state who almost singlehandedly pushed through the Indiana General Assembly a plan to restore the state's credit. This legislation, enacted in 1846 and re-enacted in a substantially different form in 1847 and known as the Butler bills, in addition to accepting the new land grant, did two major things: it assigned one half of the state's internal improvement debt to the state to be paid, principal and interest, through its tax revenues; it assigned the other half of the debt to the bondholders, who agreed not only to receive the Wabash and Erie Canal and all its properties and lands in trust, but also to raise eight hundred thousand dollars and complete the canal to Evansville.[36] Certain portions of this arrangement had been suggested by Butler at the Terre Haute and Evansville meetings, and it eventually was enacted into law. The key to the arrangement, however, was the valuable land resource in the southern district, and the key to its acceptance was the persuasiveness of Charles Butler.

Butler, whose life spanned nearly the whole of the nineteenth century, from 1802 to 1897, was a noted lawyer, churchman, and philanthropist from New York City. He served for twenty-seven years as president of the board of Union Theological Seminary, which he had helped found, and for the same number of years he was president of the Board of Trustees of the Wabash and Erie Canal Company. Slightly built and saintly in appearance, Butler was a forceful and persuasive speaker. He carried his message of morality, integrity, and the imperative need for full repayment of debt to the Indiana state legislature with true missionary zeal. He worked incessantly during both the 1845–1846 and the 1846–1847 sessions, and both times managed to propel his long and complex legislative proposals through the General Assembly.

When he arrived in Indianapolis in December, 1845, Butler's chances for success did not seem good. "The prospects are altogether discouraging and almost everybody says that *nothing* can be done," Butler confided to his wife. "Everything is merged in the most trifling local politics." A week later he added: "No man dare take the responsibility in the Legislature of advocating payment. The Governor [James Whitcomb], even though he went very far for him, yet dare not use the word *pay* or *tax*."[37] The entire responsibility of working out a settlement devolved upon Butler, who was invited to submit his proposals to the legislature.

Preparing his statement so as to offend no one but nevertheless determined to make his points emphatically, Butler was invited to read it before a joint session of the legislature on December 11, 1845. A masterpiece of subtle persuasion and logical reasoning, the paper was characterized by a "plain country member" as "first a little sugar, then a little soap, then sugar, and then soap, and it was sugar and soap all the way through."[38]

The general impression, however, was favorable, and one thousand, rather than the usual one hundred, copies were ordered printed immediately for use by the legislature and for distribution over the state. The address was referred to a joint committee of twenty-four, which studied it very carefully and worked out conflicts in conferences with Butler before drafting a bill. The essence of Butler's first proposals and the subsequent law of January, 1846, was that the state would honor its debt in full, using tax revenues to pay principal and interest on half of it. For the other half, the bondholders agreed to put up an additional $2.25 million, complete the canal to Evansville, and then look to it for repayment of the debt; but, if canal revenues failed to produce the required amounts, the state would make up the difference. Not surprisingly, however, the bondholders—Butler's employers—refused to accept this arrangement. Consequently, at the following session in 1846–1847, a second, substantially revised proposal from Butler was introduced and eventually, in January, 1847, enacted.[39]

As Logan Esarey has pointed out, the two Butler bills were quite different; the second bill of 1847 was not merely a modification of the first. Rather, it made a more complete separation of the two halves of the state debt, with the state assuming one half, and the canal revenues and properties paying the other. The bondholders accepted the second bill, agreeing to raise an additional eight hundred thousand dollars to complete the canal to Evansville. Engineering estimates had set the additional cost at $1.6 million, and the shortfall would be made up, it was hoped, from the sale of land in the Vincennes Land District.

As can be seen, the generous land grant of 1845 was the "carrot" which induced the bondholders to agree to the plan; moreover, because of the land grant, no serious consideration was given to the railroad option for the lower portion of the line. Some persons did in fact suggest this alternative,[40] but few paid any attention to it. David P. Holloway, one of the railroad men, was answered by William G. Coffin of Parke County, who insisted that no one had effectively rebutted Butler's convincing arguments in favor of the canal extension, and, in fact, accused Holloway of being an obstructionist for personal reasons; Coffin then observed that even if Holloway's arguments were true, so long as the bondholders were willing to accept the canal as payment for one half of the state's internal improvement debt, there could be no valid objection from the state. Other legislators picked up on this latter, very important point. Why should the General Assembly or anyone, they asked, oppose completion of the canal by others, at their expense? Indianans, given the federal land grants and the promise of even more land, as yet had not been taxed for it, and if the bondholders saw a potential value in the canal, it was to the state's advantage to agree with their plan.[41]

It should be remembered that up to that time no completed railroad line was in existence in the state and that the accepted mode of transport in the river valleys of the state was by water. Moreover, there were a number of ardent canal boosters in the state and in the legislature, and to them there were no real alternatives to canals. Charles Butler belonged to this group; his long supervision of the canal trust, from 1847 to 1874, was as much a labor of love and conviction in the superiority of water travel as it was a duty required of him by the bondholders whose interests he represented. It is interesting to read his concluding statements on the canal in 1874 in the last annual report of the Board of Trustees of the Wabash and Erie Canal, when the canal was in total disrepair and more resembled a series of frog ponds than a major transportation artery. Butler was still clinging to arguments urging the viability of the canal if only it were restored and asserting its usefulness not only as a common carrier but as a regulator of predatory railroads.[42]

There is time only to summarize the history of the Wabash and Erie Canal after adoption of the Butler bill of 1847. When the three-man board of trustees officially assumed control of the canal and its appurtenances in July, 1847, the enterprise was entering its most prosperous period as well as the time of its most virtuous leadership. The bondholder-elected trustees—nonresident Charles Butler and resident Thomas H. Blake of Terre Haute—were indefatigable in their labors, scrupulously honest in their dealings, and totally dedicated to making the canal a financial and commercial success.[43] High standards of performance were set for all employees, and close attention was paid both to new contract lettings and land sales on the lower divisions of the property and to efficient maintenance and operation of the canal on its upper divisions, in the belief that these were essential ingredients of successful canal management. New bookkeeping procedures and new, more modern office practices were instituted, and for a time it appeared that the trustees' conviction that honest and efficient employees and management, together with strict measures of economy and plain hard work, would be rewarded.[44]

Income from rents, tolls, and land sales was promising during the late 1840s and early 1850s—the peak year for the canal as a whole was in 1852—and slowly but steadily, despite repeated outbreaks of cholera and other epidemics among the canal laborers, the waterway inched its way through the southwestern counties of Indiana to the Ohio River at Evansville. It was clear to most observers, however, that already the canal's days were numbered; the southern extension, on which more than $2 million was spent in construction, returned less than half that much in tolls and rents during its seven partial years of operation. To the board, the reason for this was clear: it did not lie in long interruptions to navigation caused by floods and by vandalism (and there were many examples of both); rather it stemmed from the inattention, if not the perversity, of the state legislature in authorizing railroads to parallel virtually every mile of the canal during the 1850s.[45]

To the trustees, these acts violated the spirit of the 1847 agreement, and again morally obligated the state to assume direct responsibility for the entire state debt, since by its positive action the value of the canal, and hence one half of the bondholders' investment, had been destroyed. A petition specifically requesting this was submitted to the legislature in 1857, 1867, and again in 1871. The first two brought simple responses that it was "inexpedient" for the state to consider "purchase" of the canal; the third petition, however, resulted in a constitutional amendment forever prohibiting the state from recognizing obligations dating from the 1847 agreement.[46]

By then, of course, only scattered sections of the canal were in use and not long afterwards, in 1874, the trustees formally surrendered their trust and closed the books on the enterprise. The bottom lines revealed the extent of financial loss—a total of $8,259,244.03 had been spent on the Wabash and Erie Canal over the years, a total of $5,477,238.41 had been received as income. Based on these figures, many historians have agreed with Alvin F. Harlow's assessment of the failure, that it was "the most colossal, the most tragic failure in all canal history. . . ." Even Harlow, however, recognized the canal's contributions to the development of the state, adding that, "pitiable as it was, it played a tremendous part in the making of Indiana and the Middle West."[47]

In assessing the impact of canals in Indiana, I will pass over the two most widely recognized results of the internal improvement program of 1836: the bankruptcy of the state by 1839 and the consequent constitutional provision, adopted in 1851, prohibiting the state from incurring any debt, except "to meet casual deficits in the revenue; to pay the interest on the State debt; to repel invasion, suppress insurrection, or, if hostilities be threatened, provide for the public defense."[48] Instead, I will point to certain long-range developmental impacts.

Among the contemporaries who commented on the importance
of the Wabash and Erie Canal to Indiana was Calvin Fletcher of
Indianapolis. Immediately following the Fort Wayne celebration of
its opening from Lafayette to Lake Erie, he wrote an editorial for
an Indianapolis newspaper describing the novelty of sending wagons
westward (to Lafayette) with cargoes intended for eastern markets
via the new waterway, and suggesting that "the immense influence
the opening of this canal will have on three-fourths of the whole
State is incalculable."[49] Even so, he must have been surprised when
in 1844 as many as four hundred wagons a day arrived at Lafayette
with canal cargoes. It was reported that "long trains of wagons
[waited] by the hour . . . for their turns to unload" their farm
products.[50] These wagons had come as far as "100 miles to the millers
and [merchants] on the canal . . . where elevators rose and factories multiplied. . . ." In time the canal ports of Fort Wayne,
Huntington, Wabash, Peru, Logansport, Delphi, and Lafayette all
"attained a substantial commercial importance."[51] Corn shipments
at Toledo, gathered from the Wabash and Maumee valleys, grew
following the opening of the Wabash and Erie Canal from approximately 5,000 to 500,000 bushels a year, and by 1851 reached
2,775,149 bushels.[52]

Two other largely impressionistic evaluations of the canal's impact deserve mention. In 1969 Professor Charles R. Poinsatte, in his
study of *Fort Wayne during the Canal Era, 1828–1855*, concluded
that the canal had given an enormous impetus to the city's growth
by opening to the Fort Wayne market an "agricultural hinterland
which ranged from sixty miles north to Sturgis, Michigan, sixty miles
northwest to Goshen, Indiana, fifty miles south to Muncie, Indiana,
and some fifty-five miles southeast to St. Mary's, Ohio."[53] The most
elaborate analysis of canal impact, however, appears in the third and
last chapter of Elbert J. Benton, *The Wabash Trade Route* (1903).
In it he detailed the rapid growth of Indiana during the first part of
the nineteenth century, in terms both of population growth and
land value increases. Of course, he recognized other growth de-
terminants, but he pointed out, for example, that the counties border-
ing on the canal, when the first section was completed in 1835,
contained only 12,000 people. Ten years later, after the canal had
been completed from Lafayette to Toledo, the canal counties had a
population of 60,000, and in another ten years the figure stood at

150,000.[54] Additionally, industrial development—flour mills, saw mills, paper mills, and foundries, as well as grain elevators and warehouses—was promoted by and along the canal line. H. Jerome Cranmer's distinction between "developmental" and "exploitative" canals, between those designed to promote the economic development of the region and those designed to take advantage of an existing profit opportunity, is probably valid here. The Wabash and Erie Canal did not pour money into the pockets of its investors; on the other hand, its developmental impact on the state, in both the northern and southern areas, where renewed land sales and settlement had been stimulated, can be clearly seen.[55]

For their time and their place, the two Indiana canals which were completed and in operation for some twenty to forty years—the Whitewater and the Wabash and Erie canals—had a positive impact upon their regions, served to stimulate agricultural and urban growth, and helped develop the towns, the millsites, the population, and the trade which the railroads of a later time dominated so completely. This is the precise point, however, on which additional research needs to be done, and for which a careful, thorough, and sophisticated analysis of the canal impact on Indiana is needed. Fortunately, a comprehensive study of the Wabash and Erie Canal is underway (not by me but by a former resident of Logansport, now a professor of history in the South). It is to be hoped that his work will help resolve this and other still moot points in connection with what I would venture to term the single most important development in the political and economic life of Indiana during the mid-nineteenth century.

NOTES

1. The best introduction to the canal era in America remains George Rogers Taylor, *The Transportation Revolution, 1815–1860* (New York: Rinehart & Co., 1951), especially pp. 32–55. An excellent account of the origins and first decades of the Erie Canal's operation in New York is Ronald E. Shaw, *Erie Water West: A History of the Erie Canal, 1792–1854* (Lexington: University of Kentucky Press, 1966). For the origins of the Pennsylvania system and the interesting debate which surrounded it see Julius Rubin, *Canal or Railroad? Imitation and Innovation in the Response to the Erie Canal in Philadelphia, Baltimore, and Boston* (American Philosophical Society, *Transactions*, LI, Pt. 7, Philadelphia, 1961). The definitive study of the Ohio canals, set in the framework of public policy making, is Harry N. Scheiber,

Ohio Canal Era: A Case Study of Government and the Economy, 1820–1861
(Athens: Ohio University Press, 1969).

2. Dorothy Riker and Gayle Thornbrough (eds.), *Messages and Papers Relating to the Administration of Noah Noble, Governor of Indiana, 1831–1837* (*Indiana Historical Collections*, XXXVIII, Indianapolis: Indiana Historical Bureau, 1958), pp. 319–20.

3. *Laws of Indiana*, 1835–1836 (general), pp. 6–21. See also the three major sources on internal improvements in Indiana: Elbert Jay Benton, *The Wabash Trade Route in the Development of the Old Northwest* (Baltimore: Lord Baltimore Press, 1903); Logan Esarey, *Internal Improvements in Early Indiana* (Indiana Historical Society *Publications*, V, Indianapolis, 1912); and Paul Fatout, *Indiana Canals* (West Lafayette, Ind.: Purdue University Studies, 1972). Useful summaries of this act, which had such important ramifications for the state's future development, also appear in John D. Barnhart and Donald F. Carmony, *Indiana: From Frontier to Industrial Commonwealth* (4 volumes. New York: Lewis Historical Publishing Co., 1954), I, 321–27, and George S. Cottman, *Centennial History and Handbook of Indiana* (Indianapolis: M. R. Hyman, 1915), pp. 103–106. Often the figure of $13 million is cited as the amount appropriated in 1836; actually only $10 million was appropriated for the eight projects listed, but their total estimated costs did amount to approximately $13 million. See also Donald F. Carmony, "Historical Background of the Restrictions against State Debt in the Indiana Constitution of 1851," in *Indiana Magazine of History*, XLVII (1951), 129–42.

4. One of the original intentions of this paper was to review the recent literature on canals, but very little has appeared recently. In contrast to the 1960s, when a number of canal studies were published, only two such works, according to the indexes of the *Journal of American History*, appeared in the 1970s. Interestingly, one of the two dealt specifically with Indiana, the previously cited work by Paul Fatout, professor emeritus of English at Purdue University, but he made no attempt to develop a systematic method for analyzing the impact of canals upon Hoosier life.

5. Gayle Thornbrough (ed.), *The Correspondence of John Badollet and Albert Gallatin, 1804–1836* (Indiana Historical Society *Publications*, XXII, Indianapolis, 1963), pp. 48–49.

6. See, for example, Isaac J. Cox, "The Burr Conspiracy in Indiana," in *Indiana Magazine of History*, XXV (1929), 258–69; and Fatout, *Indiana Canals*, p. 6.

7. Fatout, *Indiana Canals*, p. 21.

8. *Ibid.*, pp. 2–21; Esarey, *Internal Improvements*, pp. 65–69; Paul B. Trescott, "The Louisville and Portland Canal Company, 1825–1874," in *Mississippi Valley Historical Review*, XLIV (1958), 689–708; and Carter Goodrich, *Government Promotion of American Canals and Railroads, 1800–1890* (New York: Columbia University Press, 1960), pp. 40, 42, 169, 273. For an analysis of William Hendricks's long efforts as congressman, governor, and senator to obtain an Ohio falls canal on the Indiana side of the river see Frederick D. Hill, "William Hendricks: Indiana Politician and Western

Advocate, 1812–1850" (Ph.D. dissertation, Indiana University, 1972), pp. 42–46, 87–92, 163–64, 220–24.

9. The classic account of this portage route, as well as an early and valuable study of the Wabash and Erie Canal, is Benton, *The Wabash Trade Route*.

10. Quoted in *ibid.*, p. 33.

11. See Harlow Lindley (ed.), *Indiana as Seen by Early Travelers: A Collection of Reprints from Books of Travel, Letters and Diaries prior to 1830 (Indiana Historical Collections*, III, Indianapolis: Indiana Historical Bureau, 1916), p. 243; Logan Esarey (ed.), *Messages and Papers of Jonathan Jennings, Ratliff Boon, William Hendricks (Indiana Historical Collections*, XII, Indianapolis: Indiana Historical Bureau, 1924); and, for the Clinton statement Frederick Jackson Turner, *The United States, 1830–1850: The Nation and Its Sections* (New York: H. Holt and Co., 1935), p. 313.

12. See Taylor, *The Transportation Revolution*, and Goodrich, *Government Promotion of American Canals and Railroads*. An eastern canal company became, in 1825, the first to receive federal aid in the form of a stock subscription. For the story of its long struggle to obtain the grant see Ralph D. Gray, *The National Waterway: A History of the Chesapeake and Delaware Canal, 1769–1965* (Urbana: University of Illinois Press, 1967), pp. 22–42, 53–55.

13. *Congressional Debates*, 19 Cong., 1 Sess., 591–97, and 19 Cong., 2 Sess., 311–12, 337; Frederick D. Hill (ed.), "William Hendricks' Political Circulars to his Constituents: First Senatorial Term, 1826–1831," in *Indiana Magazine of History*, LXXI (1975), 124–80. Hendricks was responsible for the creation of the Senate's Select Committee on Roads and Canals each session from 1825 to 1829, and he served as its chairman each term. In 1830 Roads and Canals became a standing committee of the Senate.

14. See John Bell Rae, "Federal Land Grants in Aid of Canals," in *Journal of Economic History*, IV (1944), 167–77; Goodrich, *Government Promotion of American Canals and Railroads*; and Benjamin Horace Hibbard, *A History of the Public Land Policies* (1924, reprinted Madison: University of Wisconsin Press, 1965), pp. 228–68.

15. Fatout, *Indiana Canals*, p. 39.

16. *Ibid.*, pp. 47–48, 101–109. The Wabash and Erie joined the Miami and Erie Canal at Junction, Ohio, just south of Defiance. For the remaining distance to Toledo and Lake Erie, the two canals shared the same route.

17. Dorothy Riker and Gayle Thornbrough (eds.), *Messages and Papers Relating to the Administration of James Brown Ray, Governor of Indiana, 1825–1831 (Indiana Historical Collections*, XXXIV, Indianapolis: Indiana Historical Bureau, 1954), pp. 278–80.

18. Indiana *Senate Journal*, 1827–1828, p. 77.

19. Fatout, *Indiana Canals*, p. 70. See also the December 17, 1831, report of the commissioners of the Wabash and Erie Canal which includes statements on the relative merits of canals and railroads. Indiana *House Journal*, 1831–1832, Appendix F, and a discussion of the same issue in Indiana *House Journal*, 1834–1835, pp. 346–49.

20. Indianapolis *Indiana Journal*, June 14, 1834.

21. The Wabash and Erie Canal was formally abandoned by the trustees in 1874; Jesse L. Williams, who had become chief engineer of the canal at age twenty-four, died in 1886.

22. Logansport *Canal Telegraph*, December 2, 1835. The editor had only recently changed the name of his newspaper in anticipation of future greatness for both the paper and the canal, and he carried full reports on internal improvement issues and the progress of legislation regarding them in his paper. The front page of the January 30, 1836, issue was entirely devoted to printing in full the "general system" act just adopted. For the Fort Wayne canal celebration see *Canal Celebrations in Old Fort Wayne* (Fort Wayne, 1953), a booklet compiled by the staff of the Fort Wayne-Allen County Public Library.

23. Barnhart and Carmony, *Indiana*, I, 322, 324.

24. Gayle Thornbrough *et al.* (eds.), *The Diary of Calvin Fletcher* (8 volumes to date. Indianapolis: Indiana Historical Society, 1972—), I, 299. Fletcher eventually came to look upon the unfinished portions of the state system in central Indiana with increasing disgust. See, for example, Fletcher's comments of March 29, 1840, *ibid.*, II, 167. Later, of course, Democratic politicians attempted to fix responsibility for the internal improvement embarrassments of the state upon the Whigs. See especially Jacob P. Chapman's twelve-part series on the history of internal improvements in Indiana told from an extreme partisan viewpoint. The articles appeared during the 1843 election "canvass" in the Indianapolis *Indiana State Sentinel* between April 4 and July 4, 1843.

25. Chelsea L. Lawlis, "Settlement and Economic Development of the Whitewater Valley, 1800–1900" (Ph.D. dissertation, Indiana University, 1956), pp. 162–204; Harry O. Garman, *Whitewater Canal, Cambridge City to Ohio River: A Pioneer Transportation Facility in Indiana Constructed 1836 to 1847* (n.p., 1944).

26. Esarey, *Internal Improvements*, p. 123. See also Rick Stout, "Indiana's Central Canal," in *Outdoor Indiana*, XXXIII (1968), 30–32. For an early statement on the need, purpose, and usefulness of the canal see "Memorial and Resolution of Indiana, on the Subject of a Canal in the Valley of White River," *Senate Documents*, 23 Cong., 2 Sess., No. 143. The state was also seeking a land grant of five sections per mile of canal for this waterway.

27. See Fatout, *Indiana Canals*, pp. 98–99, for a compilation of the work done by 1839. It totaled 129 miles of canal, 28 of railroad, and 41 of turnpike, all at a cost of approximately $8 million. Later Hoosiers talked about "infernal improvements," told new jokes about the Indiana General Assembly—Question: "What General ruled the legislature?" Answer: "General Panic"—and attempted to assign party responsibility for the 1836 act. The outspoken editor of the *Indiana State Sentinel*, Democrat Jacob P. Chapman, manfully admitted that some Democrats had voted for the bill, but he still called it a "Whig system" passed by a "Whig legislature," a view that many Indiana voters seemed to accept. *Indiana State Sentinel*, January 6, 1846. The Democrats

regained control of the state government in 1843 and remained in power until 1860.

28. Fatout, *Indiana Canals*, p. 104.

29. The scrip could be turned over to the state in payment for taxes, land, or tolls on the Wabash and Erie Canal. *Ibid.*, pp. 102, 108, 143.

30. *Ibid.*, pp. 104–105.

31. *Ibid.*, p. 110.

32. *Ibid.* See also the historical article by Leroy Armstrong in the Lafayette *Weekly Journal*, September 15, 1899.

33. None of the three major secondary accounts of the canal—Benton, Esarey, or Fatout—emphasizes this third land grant; indeed, only Fatout clearly distinguishes it from the previous donations, but he draws no special implications from it. Fatout, *Indiana Canals*, p. 109.

34. See "Report of the Committee on Public Lands," *Senate Documents*, 28 Cong., 1 Sess., No. 202. To this report was appended a letter to the committee from Senator Albert S. White reviewing the history and current status of the Wabash and Erie Canal.

35. Fatout, *Indiana Canals*, p. 109. For an excellent summary of the complicated legislative history of the canal land grants see "Wabash and Erie Canal Lands," a report compiled by the staff of the Archives Division, Commission on Public Records, Indiana State Library and Historical Building.

36. Esarey, *Internal Improvements*, pp. 135–43; Fatout, *Indiana Canals*, pp. 114–15, 120–25. See also G. L. Prentiss, *The Union Theological Seminary in the City of New York: Its Design and Another Decade of Its History. With a Sketch of the Life and Public Services of Charles Butler, LL.D.* (Asbury Park, N.J.: M., W. & C. Pennypacker, 1899), which contains long extracts of Butler's correspondence to his family during his first winter in Indianapolis, 1845–1846. An indication of the public dissatisfaction with Indiana's long failure to honor its debt can be found in the contemporary press. A Whitewater Valley resident, in urging passage of the Butler bill, admitted that "I am really beginning to feel it is a disgrace to be an Indianian." Indianapolis *Indiana State Sentinel*, January 5, 1846. For a report on the Evansville canal meeting see *ibid.*, December 25, 1845. The delegates had recommended completion of the canal as the "only reliable means" of extinguishing the state debt.

37. Prentiss, *The Union Theological Seminary*, pp. 454, 456.

38. *Ibid.*, p. 464. Butler added that members of the Indiana General Assembly used very little of the latter commodity.

39. Esarey, *Internal Improvements*, p. 139.

40. See, for example, the Indianapolis *Indiana Journal*, December 10, 1845. A Kentucky correspondent suggested that the Indiana legislature, in accepting the grant of lands to complete its "great national canal," would have the "good sense" to call upon Congress for its consent to change the lower line of the route from a canal to a railroad, "as they now have the decided preference everywhere."

41. *Ibid.*, December 29, 1845.

42. *Annual Report of the Board of Trustees of the Wabash and Erie Canal*, 1874 (Indianapolis, 1875), pp. 6–9.

43. The state appointed the third trustee. A total of twelve different people filled this appointive position, whereas only three persons were elected by the bondholders to serve as trustees. Thomas H. Blake, a former member of the Indiana General Assembly and a former Commissioner of the General Land Office, became a victim of the cholera outbreak on the canal in 1849. He was replaced in 1850 by Thomas Dowling, also of Terre Haute, who served throughout the life of the board with Charles Butler. *Ibid.*, p. 9.

44. Letter Book No. 1, 1847–1850, Board of Trustees of the Wabash and Erie Canal, Wabash and Erie Canal Papers, Archives Division, Commission on Public Records, Indiana State Library and Historical Building.

45. *Annual Report of the Board of Trustees of the Wabash and Erie Canal*, 1858 (Indianapolis, 1859), pp. [3–7].

46. Charles Kettleborough (ed.), *Constitution Making in Indiana: A Source Book of Constitutional Documents with Historical Introduction and Critical Notes* (*Indiana Historical Collections*, I, II, XVII, Indianapolis: Indiana Historical Bureau, 1916–1930), II, 105–106.

47. Alvin F. Harlow, *Old Towpaths: The Story of the American Canal Era* (New York: D. Appleton and Co., 1926), p. 278.

48. Kettleborough (ed.), *Constitution Making in Indiana*, I, 352. Additional restrictions were imposed upon counties by the Constitution, which prohibited them from giving credit or buying stock in corporations except upon cash terms. For a full discussion of the 1851 Constitution see Barnhart and Carmony, *Indiana*, II, 83–104.

49. Thornbrough *et al.* (eds.), *The Diary of Calvin Fletcher*, II, 510, 511n.

50. George S. Cottman, "Internal Improvements in Indiana, No. III: The Wabash and Erie Canal," in *Indiana Magazine of History*, III (1907), 105.

51. Lafayette *Weekly Journal*, September 15, 1899.

52. Benton, *The Wabash Trade Route*, p. 99.

53. Charles R. Poinsatte, *Fort Wayne during the Canal Era, 1828–1855* (*Indiana Historical Collections*, XLVI, Indianapolis: Indiana Historical Bureau, 1969), p. 239.

54. Benton, *The Wabash Trade Route*, p. 95.

55. H. Jerome Cranmer, "Improvements without Public Funds: The New Jersey Canals," in Carter Goodrich (ed.), *Canals and American Economic Development* (New York: Columbia University Press, 1961), p. 157; cf. Roger L. Ransom, "Public Canal Investment and the Opening of the Old Northwest," in David C. Klingaman and Richard K. Vedder (eds.), *Essays in Nineteenth Century Economic History: The Old Northwest* (Athens: Ohio University Press, 1975), pp. 246–68.

Iron Roads in the Old Northwest: The Railroads and the Growing Nation

John F. Stover

In the last half dozen years the nation has celebrated the sesqui-centennial of the first railroad construction and service in the United States. It is rather difficult to be certain of "firsts" when rival states, communities, or railroads each claim to have built or operated the "first railroad." In February, 1825, Colonel John Stevens entertained his more venturesome houseguests when he let them ride on his sixteen-foot "Steam Waggon" locomotive running at a speed of perhaps twelve miles an hour around the circular track located on his estate at Hoboken, New Jersey. A year and a half later Gridley Bryant, a Massachusetts inventor and civil engineer, opened his broad-gauge Granite Railway at Quincy for the transportation of granite to build the Bunker Hill Monument. And in 1829, in Hones-dale, Pennsylvania, Horatio Allen, the resident engineer of the Delaware and Hudson Canal and Railroad Company, tried out an English-built locomotive, the *Stourbridge Lion*. Allen soon discovered that the seven-ton engine was too heavy and rigid for American track.[1]

Regular rail service for the American public was introduced by the Baltimore and Ohio Railroad, a line incorporated by Baltimore merchants early in 1827 and started on July 4, 1828. By late May, 1830, thirteen miles of track running out to Ellicott's Mills, Mary-land, were being operated by horses pulling "rail wagons" and giving passenger and freight service to the public. The B and O service thus predated by six months the first service of the *Best Friend of Charles-*

John F. Stover is Emeritus Professor of History in Purdue University.

ton on Christmas Day, 1830, and by more than a year the first steam train in New York state, pulled by the *DeWitt Clinton*.[2]

New England was a bit laggard with early rail construction, but by 1835 three lines were in operation out of Boston. By 1841 Boston was served by a 150-mile transectional line which crossed the state to connect with the Erie Canal at Albany. But the new Western Railroad never obtained much of the canal traffic, which instead went down the Hudson to New York City. Most Bostonians were forced to agree with Charles F. Adams, Jr., who would later write that the Western Railroad was built upon "the fallacy that steam could run uphill cheaper than water could run down."[3] But the Yankees continued to construct rail mileage, and by 1850 New England was far better supplied with railways than any other region in the nation.

In the score of years prior to 1850 the five mid-Atlantic states also built much rail mileage. This was especially true in New York and Pennsylvania. By mid-century the Empire State had nearly completed two rail routes to Lake Erie, the Central Line consisting of ten little railroads strung along the Mohawk Valley and the Erie Canal, and the New York and Erie running through the southern counties of the state to Dunkirk. By mid-century J. Edgar Thomson was building the Pennsylvania Railroad over and through the high Alleghenies from Harrisburg to Pittsburgh. By 1850 over 5,600 miles of railroad—three fifths of the national total—were located in the northeastern region, the New England and the mid-Atlantic states. In the eleven-state area, New York was first with 1,361 miles, Pennsylvania second with 1,240 miles, and Massachusetts third with 1,035 miles.[4]

South of the Potomac and Ohio rivers, railroads were much less common than in the Northeast. In 1850 southern states could claim just over 2,100 miles of lines, or about 23 percent of the national rail system. Georgia with 643 miles and Virginia with 481 miles had almost half of the southern total. In 1850 the network of lines serving Virginia and North Carolina did not connect with the roads located in Georgia and South Carolina. North of the Ohio River each of the five states of the Old Northwest had some rail mileage at mid-century, but only Ohio had as much as 500 miles of line. Neither Ohio nor any of the other states north of the Ohio River had rail connections with any of their neighboring states. The railroad system serving the nation in 1850 was in reality little more than a skimpy network from Maine to Maryland, with a scattering of additional lines to the South and West.[5]

During the early years of railroad operation, most railways had much larger passenger than freight revenues, but by 1850 passenger and freight revenues were about equal on most lines. The nine thousand miles of railroad in 1850 lacked many of the features and characteristics which later would provide the nation with an efficient railway system. No one had yet introduced the telegraph for the control of train movements. Track gauge—the distance between the rails, measured from inside to inside—varied in the different regions of the nation. It would be many years before the English 4-foot, 8½-inch gauge would become standard for the nation. In 1850 few rivers of any size were spanned by railway bridges: no railroad bridge yet spanned the middle or lower Ohio, the Niagara, the middle or lower Hudson, or the Potomac in the vicinity of Washington, D.C.

The lack of rail passenger service west of the nation's capital in March, 1849, can be seen as a forty-year-old former congressman traveled home to his law practice in Illinois. Even though his wife was back in Springfield, Abraham Lincoln did not immediately return home following the inauguration of President Zachary Taylor on March 5, 1849. The records are sketchy, but Lincoln probably left Washington on March 20 or March 21, 1849, taking eleven or twelve days to return to Illinois by railroad, stagecoach, and steamboat.

An all-day train trip over the Washington Branch of the Baltimore and Ohio line to the Relay House (west of Baltimore) and then the B and O "great western mail" on to Cumberland, Maryland, covered about two hundred miles for a total fare of $8.60. Cumberland had been the "end of track" for the Baltimore and Ohio for several years. At Cumberland the lanky Illinois lawyer transferred to one of several stage lines which crossed the steep mountain grades of Maryland and Pennsylvania west to Wheeling on the upper Ohio. The 130-mile stage journey took about twenty-four hours, and a ticket in the nine-passenger, Concord-type coach cost the homeward-bound congressman another $4.00 to $5.00. At Wheeling Lincoln boarded a steamboat for the 1,100-mile river journey down the Ohio to Cairo and up the Mississippi to Saint Louis. At mid-century Saint Louis had an average of eight or nine steamboat arrivals from the Ohio each week. The returning congressman reached Saint Louis by March 26, 1849, and a few days later he was home in Springfield.⁶

The ease of western travel would increase during the 1850s. The long decade between the Mexican War and the firing on Fort Sumter was to be a period of dynamic growth for America. The population in 1850, just over 23 million, represented a record 36 percent increase for the decade, the highest growth rate in forty years. By 1850 "Manifest Destiny" was a reality, and Americans were proud of new maps which revealed their western borders to be on the Rio Grande and the far Pacific. The decade of the fifties was prosperous for both farm and factory, and the nation enjoyed an unparalleled expansion of its material wealth and resources. Foreign trade grew in the decade, but the internal commerce expanded even faster.

All these factors hastened railroad construction, and between 1850 and 1860 the rail mileage increased from 9,021 to 30,626 miles. Each of the ten years—1851 through 1860—saw at least 1,300 miles of new track laid, and in 1856 more than 3,600 miles were constructed. Early in 1857 the *American Railroad Journal* reported that the United States had 24,500 miles of railway out of a world total of 51,000. With only 5 percent of the world's population, the nation was building railroads nearly as fast as the rest of the world together.⁷

During the 1850s, western states built nearly 10,000 miles of railroad, far more than either the South or the Northeast. During the decade, New England increased its iron network by only 46 percent, the mid-Atlantic states little more than doubled their rail mileage, and the southern states increased their rail system by nearly 350 percent. Between 1850 and 1860 western states increased their rail mileage more than sevenfold. The amount of new railroad construction in Ohio, 2,371 miles, was twice the total for the six states of New England, while Illinois and Indiana together, with 4,613 new miles of road, built more than were added in the five mid-Atlantic states in the decade. The four states directly west of Pennsylvania— Ohio, Indiana, Illinois, and Iowa—together added 7,640 miles of new railroad, more than was constructed in the twelve southern states (the Confederate states plus Kentucky) during the 1850s.⁸

About 85 percent of the 9,800 miles of new western mileage

constructed in the fifties was located in the five states of the Old Northwest. In 1860 the only western rail mileage beyond the Mississippi was found in Iowa with 655 miles of track; Missouri, 817 miles; and California, 23 miles. In 1850 only one western state, Ohio, had over 500 miles of railroad. Ten years later, all but one of the western states with operating railroads had well over 500 miles in service.

In 1850 New York, Pennsylvania, and Massachusetts ranked respectively first, second, and third in rail mileage in the nation. On the eve of the Civil War the same three states were only third, fourth, and eighth in the national ranking. Ohio ranked only fifth in rail mileage in 1850. By 1860 the Buckeye State, with 2,946 miles of railroad, was first among all the states. Illinois in 1850, with only two short roads running west of Springfield and west of Chicago, had only 111 miles of line and ranked eighteenth in the nation. Ten years later, her 2,790 miles of railroad placed her second in mileage, just behind Ohio. The five-state area had over 9,500 miles of railroad in 1860. Behind Ohio and Illinois, Indiana, with 2,163 miles, ranked fifth, while Wisconsin ranked twelfth, and Michigan fifteenth in the nation.

Henry V. Poor, who became editor of the *American Railroad Journal* in 1849, was quick to note the rising enthusiasm for railroads in the West. He wrote an editorial in the fall of 1850:

> The public feeling in the West, upon the subject of railroads, is excited to an extraordinary degree. The people of every town and county in the great valley, are now putting forth all their means to secure to themselves the advantages of railroads. . . . The west is now the great theatre of railroading in this country.[9]

Money as well as mileage was involved in the hectic railroad construction in the West. The eleven thousand miles of western rail mileage in 1860 represented a total investment of about $390 million and amounted to nearly half of all new rail capital in the decade. Western mileage built in the 1850s cost an average of over $36,000 per mile, a bit below the national average. On the eve of the Civil War the average investment was nearly $48,000 per mile for the eleven New England and mid-Atlantic states, while the more lightly built lines in the twelve southern states had an average cost of only $27,000 per mile.

Western railroads were generally longer than those in eastern and southern states. The 113 western lines listed in the 1860 census averaged 98 miles in length. In the South the 115 lines averaged 83 miles in length, while the 235 separate roads in the eleven mid-Atlantic and New England states had a much shorter average length of only 43 miles. In 1860 there were 41 railroads more than 100 miles in length in western states. All but 5 of these longer lines were located in the Old Northwest, and 39 of them were located in the three states of Ohio, Indiana, and Illinois.[10]

In 1850 Ohio already had several operating railroads and, with 575 miles of line, ranked fifth in mileage among the states. At mid-century the railroads of Ohio ran north and south, connecting the two Lake Erie ports of Cleveland and Sandusky with Columbus in the central part of the state and Cincinnati on the Ohio River. Alfred Kelley, one of Cleveland's first lawyers and a longtime member of the state legislature, was president of two of Ohio's five railways. In the 1820s and 1830s Kelley had been a prime mover in planning and building the Ohio system of canals, a network of waterways that reached a total of 740 miles by 1840. By the late 1840s Alfred Kelley had shifted his allegiance to railroads. Kelley was the man of whom Henry Clay was reported to have said: "He had too much cast-iron in his composition to be popular." Popular or not, Kelley still had the leadership to meet the opposition of interests in western Pennsylvania as he built a line from Cleveland eastward along the lake shore to connect with the Erie and New York Central lines in western New York State. Kelley's railroad would later become a major portion of the Lake Shore Line of the New York Central.[11]

Nearly all of the major lines built in Ohio during the decade would ultimately be controlled by one of three major eastern trunk lines: the New York Central, the Pennsylvania, and the Baltimore and Ohio. Of the five Ohio lines that eventually would come under the control of the Pennsylvania, the most important was the Pittsburgh, Fort Wayne and Chicago. This road was built across northern Ohio, via Alliance, Crestline, and Lima, and was completed to the Ohio-Indiana line during 1854. The president of the Pittsburgh, Fort Wayne and Chicago in the mid-fifties was George Washington Cass, nephew of Lewis Cass, active Democratic political leader and later Secretary of State under James Buchanan. During the late mid-1850s, two railroads with financial connections to the Baltimore and Ohio were built from Bellaire and Marietta, Ohio River towns, westward to Cincinnati.[12]

Most of the rail construction in the Buckeye State during the fifties was from east to west. By the eve of the Civil War, there were four lines across the Ohio-Pennsylvania border, and seven across the Ohio-Indiana state line. The bulk of the Ohio track was laid in the 4-foot, 10-inch gauge, but some mileage in the northern and southern parts of the state was the standard 4-foot, 8½-inch gauge.

The eighty-six-mile Madison and Indianapolis Railroad was the major completed rail line in Indiana at mid-century. This railroad had been started in the late 1830s as a part of the ambitious Indiana Internal Improvement Program. Completion of the line to Indianapolis in 1847 was made possible by loans from James F. D. Lanier, a Madison banker, who later would help Indiana with its financial problems during the Civil War. When the first train arrived in Indianapolis on October 1, 1847, Stoughton Fletcher, sixteen-year-old son of Calvin Fletcher, a banker-lawyer of Indianapolis, obtained a free ride on the cars "by assisting the enginear by handing a bucket of water at intervals." By the early 1850s the Madison and Indianapolis had a small debt and sufficient traffic to pay good dividends. By the late 1850s the new Union Depot at Indianapolis was becoming the rail hub of the state, with seven lines radiating out from the city.[13]

Indiana, like Ohio, was served by western extensions of several eastern trunk line railroads. Two such roads in the northern part of the state were the Michigan Southern and Northern Indiana, and the Michigan Central, a pair of Michigan lines running respectively from Monroe and Detroit towards Lake Michigan and Chicago. The Michigan Southern and Northern Indiana was built through Elkhart and LaPorte by George Bliss and John B. Jervis, two railroaders from the East, and reached Chicago by the spring of 1852. That same spring a trio of Yankees from New England, John Murray Forbes, John W. Brooks, and James F. Joy, extended their Michigan Central from Michigan City to the tracks of the Illinois Central, which gave entry into Chicago. Both of the Michigan roads were eventually merged into the New York Central.[14]

Farther south, two other westward-looking lines were to cross the state via Fort Wayne. The Ohio and Indiana Railroad, later to become part of the Pittsburgh, Fort Wayne and Chicago and partially financed by J. Edgar Thomson and his Pennsylvania Railroad, was opened for traffic to Fort Wayne in November, 1854. Additional money from the Pennsylvania permitted the road to be built to Plymouth in 1856, and on into Chicago by the end of 1858. The second line serving Fort Wayne in the 1850s was the 243-mile Toledo, Wabash and Western. This road was built from Toledo to Fort Wayne in 1855, and the following year it was continued westward via Peru, Logansport, and Lafayette to the Illinois state line. Even though the line ran parallel to the Wabash and Erie Canal through much of its route, its traffic by the late fifties included twice as much freight revenue as passenger.[15]

The Ohio and Mississippi, a third major east-west line, crossed southern Indiana from Cincinnati to Vincennes, continuing on to East Saint Louis. This 340-mile road was chartered in three states: in Indiana on February 14, 1848; in Ohio on March 15, 1849; and in Illinois on February 12, 1851. Included among the early sponsors of the O and M were Alphonso Taft, Cincinnati lawyer and father of a later American president, Judge Abner T. Ellis of Vincennes, an early sponsor of river traffic on the Wabash, and John O'Fallon, soldier-merchant of Saint Louis and nephew of George Rogers Clark.

Cincinnati, a city of 115,000 at mid-century, was eager to have a rail connection with Saint Louis, and in 1849 its citizens voted to have their city subscribe to a million dollars of stock. Despite such support, construction was slow. In 1854 a 27-mile segment was built west of Cincinnati, and a 61-mile stretch was completed in southwestern Illinois. In 1855 the road was extended 100 miles to Mitchell, Indiana, and another 87 miles were built in Illinois. Early in 1857 the final 65-mile segment in Indiana, from Mitchell west to Vincennes, was built, and the entire line was finished. The rail mileage from Cincinnati to Saint Louis was roughly half the river steamer distance via the Ohio and Mississippi.[16]

The completed Ohio and Mississippi was a natural westward extension of both the Marietta and Cincinnati and the Baltimore and Ohio. The three roads together provided a new 900-mile through line from Baltimore to Saint Louis. Chauncey Brooks, president of the Baltimore and Ohio since 1855, decided that a giant excursion from Baltimore to Saint Louis was the only proper way to celebrate the opening of this new "American Central Route." The guest lists, special trains, banquets, and speechmaking were all reminiscent of the festivities which had earlier marked the completion of the Erie Railroad in 1851.

President James Buchanan was unable to accept Chauncey Brooks's invitation, but Secretary of State Lewis Cass, Henry Ward Beecher, George Bancroft, and many lesser notables joined the excursion, which left Baltimore in several trains on June 1, 1857. Overnight stops were made at Grafton, Virginia, and Chillicothe, Ohio, prior to the arrival at Cincinnati. The citizens of Cincinnati marked the celebration with more speeches, marching bands, and demonstrations by several rival fire companies showing off their new equipment. Somehow a careless fire crew threw a stream of water into a carriage, dousing the Secretary of State and sending his fine silk hat into a Cincinnati gutter.[17]

One of the longer Indiana lines was the New Albany and Salem, which by the eve of the Civil War was reorganized as the Louisville, New Albany and Chicago. Chartered in 1847 to connect two southern towns in Indiana, by 1851 the line had been built from New Albany, across from Louisville, Kentucky, through Salem to Orleans, 57 miles to the northwest. James Brooks, a visionary New Albany businessman, was the president of the road. Brooks insisted that his short southern line should be extended north to Lake Michigan. During 1853 a 119-mile section of road was built from Crawfordsville north to Michigan City, and the following year almost as much was added as the gap was closed between Orleans and Crawfordsville. The entire 288-mile road from the Ohio to Lake Michigan was completed with the laying of the last rail on June 24, 1854.[18]

The dominant gauge of the Hoosier rail network in the fifties was the standard 4-foot, 8½-inch gauge. However, the Ohio and Mississippi's track was laid in the broad 6-foot gauge, and several lines in the northern half of the state followed the pattern of Ohio in being built in the 4-foot, 10-inch gauge.

Illinois in 1850 had only two short rail lines, with a total of just over a hundred miles. However, during the 1850s the state constructed more track than any other state in the nation. Only two of the major railroads in the state later came under the control of eastern trunk lines. This was true because so many of the Illinois lines were built to serve the growing western trade of Chicago. Standard gauge track was universal in Illinois except for the broad gauge Ohio and Mississippi.

The Illinois Central, the first railroad in the nation to receive a land grant, was probably the most important of the major rail lines serving Illinois and Chicago. Chartered in 1851, the Illinois Central was projected in the shape of a thin wishbone running the length of the state from Dunleith and Chicago in the north down to Cairo at the junction of the Ohio and Mississippi rivers. Many observers contended that the Illinois Central was being built the "wrong way" since most projected lines in the upper Mississippi Valley ran from east to west to capture the trade of the expanding frontier.

Construction of the Illinois Central was started in 1853 under the direction of Colonel Roswell B. Mason, engineer-in-chief. Borrowed money plus the orderly sale of almost half the 2.5 million-acre land grant permitted a steady construction of the line, and the entire road was finished in September, 1856. During the mid-fifties the cost of living was rising, and a bushel of potatoes or a gallon of whiskey might cost 40 to 50 cents in Illinois. Before the road was finished, Mason was having to pay $1.50 a day to the German and Irish workers in his track gangs. When completed, the 705-mile Illinois Central was reported to be the longest railroad in the world. The strongest of the early presidents of the Illinois Central was William H. Osborn, a New Englander who quickly became a vigorous and dedicated railroad executive.[19]

Three other important Illinois roads were the Chicago and Northwestern, the Chicago and Rock Island, and the Chicago, Burlington and Quincy. All three served Chicago, and before the Civil War all three were building western extensions across the Mississippi to seek out the trade of Iowa and Missouri. The first railroad to serve Chicago was the Galena and Chicago Union, which during the Civil War would come under the control of the Chicago and Northwestern. William Butler Ogden, Chicago's first mayor and a well-to-do real estate man, was the prime mover of the Galena and Chicago Union. Ogden initially found little financial support in Chicago for the road, but farmers living along the proposed route helped fill the first subscription books, and by 1848 Chicago had its first railroad. In 1850 the forty-two-mile road from Chicago to Elgin was grossing one thousand dollars a week. Later, Ogden became interested in other Chicago-based lines projected into Wisconsin. These roads were reorganized in 1859 as the Chicago and

Northwestern, which five years later acquired the Galena and Chicago Union.[20]

The Chicago and Rock Island, another major line connecting Chicago and the Mississippi, was the first road to bridge successfully the "Father of the Waters." The line was chartered on February 7, 1851, by the Illinois state legislature, and construction west of Chicago was pushed vigorously. Track was laid to Joliet, 40 miles west of Chicago, by October, 1852. The entire 181-mile road was completed to Rock Island, on the Mississippi, by June, 1854, the same year that Henry Farnam, self-taught surveyor, was elected president of the line. By 1856 Farnam had completed the railroad bridge across the Mississippi, which carried the tracks of his railroad into Davenport, Iowa.[21]

Once the Michigan Central reached Chicago in 1852, John Murray Forbes and his associates turned their attention to the acquisition and construction of connecting lines from Chicago to the Mississippi and beyond. By 1855 Forbes, John W. Brooks, and James F. Joy had organized the Chicago, Burlington and Quincy, a line which soon was providing rail service from Chicago to two points on the Mississippi River—Burlington, Iowa, and Quincy, Illinois. Soon Forbes's group was financing lines west of Burlington and Quincy into the prairie lands of Iowa and Missouri.[22]

The iron network of Illinois and the other states of the Midwest favored some cities more than others. In 1852 James DeBow wrote that Cincinnati and Saint Louis would become "the primary cities of the central United States." The rapid growth of Chicago and its rail network built in the 1850s was to prove him wrong. In 1857 the *Missouri Democrat*, published in Chicago's rival city, Saint Louis, admitted that the granaries, storehouses, and railroad depots of Chicago were "scarcely surpassed by any city in the Union." In 1860 Chicago was a city of 109,000, with eleven different railroads; boosters claimed that one hundred trains a day served their city. Chicago was indeed the major rail terminal of the new east-west rail network, a system described by Horace Greeley as "long iron arms extending far into the productive west."[23]

On the eve of the Civil War, Michigan had nearly eight hundred miles of railroad, while the iron network in Wisconsin was just over nine hundred miles. Railroad building in both states in the 1850s was less hectic than in Ohio, Indiana, and Illinois. These two northern states were somewhat cut off from trunk line rail projects because of their proximity to the Great Lakes. The two major Michigan lines, the Michigan Central and the Michigan Southern and Northern Indiana, were already constructed nearly across the southern counties of the state in 1850. The third important road in Michigan, the 188-mile Detroit and Milwaukee, was built across the state to Grand Haven on Lake Michigan between 1855 and 1858.

As in Michigan, most of the railroad construction in Wisconsin during the fifties was headed west, specifically from ports on Lake Michigan to the Mississippi River. The major rail promoter in Milwaukee was Mayor Bryon Kilbourn, who had earlier been interested in canals and plank roads both in Ohio and Michigan. Kilbourn's dream of Milwaukee's rail empire was revealed by a map on his office wall which showed future rail lines connecting Milwaukee with LaCross, Dubuque, Saint Paul, and western points beyond.

With help from hundreds of Wisconsin farmers who mortgaged their farms to purchase stock in his railroad, Kilbourn—between 1851 and 1857—built the 234-mile Milwaukee and Mississippi westward to Prairie du Chien on the Mississippi. Between 1855 and 1858, Kilbourn built the 200-mile La Crosse and Milwaukee, a road also largely financed with stock bought after owners mortgaged their farms. By the late fifties, both of Kilbourn's roads were near bankruptcy, and hundreds of Wisconsin farmers were about to face foreclosure proceedings.[24]

But even with some failures and disappointments, the overall picture for the decade was one of major achievements. More than twenty thousand miles of new line had been built in the 1850s, nearly half of it in the western states north of the Ohio River. What at mid-century had been little more than a scattering of short and incomplete lines stretching from Maine to Georgia had become, by 1860, an iron network serving all the states east of the Mississippi. During the decade, the railroad industry had grown and matured. Few other economic institutions of that day did business on so vast a scale, obtained their financial support from such a variety of sources, or employed so many workers of diverse skills. The westward push of rail construction by the eve of the Civil War had placed many railroads very near the moving edge of the frontier in mid-America.

In 1849 Abraham Lincoln had taken a long and slow journey

home to Springfield from Washington, D.C. The fifteen hundred-mile trip had been accomplished far more by riverboat and stagecoach than by railroad car. The decade of the 1850s had been years of expanding legal and political activity for Lincoln, and in 1860 he was elected the sixteenth president of the United States. Three weeks before his inauguration, on a drizzling Monday morning, February 11, 1861, Lincoln boarded a special train at Springfield to start a twelve-day trip to Washington. Lincoln spent the morning of his fifty-second birthday in Indianapolis, the first of nine cities where he made an overnight stop. The prolonged and roundabout trip (nineteen hundred miles over twenty railroads in eight states) to Washington was aimed more to generate political goodwill than to ensure Lincoln's speedy arrival in Washington.[25]

In February, 1861, Lincoln certainly could have traveled by rail far more easily and quickly than a dozen years earlier. If the president-elect, after reaching Cincinnati from Indianapolis, had taken the Marietta and Cincinnati to Parkersburg and then the B and O, his rail trip to Washington would have taken only two days for the 966-mile trip. When Abraham Lincoln traveled east to take the presidential oath of office, he could have taken any of seven east-west rail lines that crossed the Illinois-Indiana border, any of seven that crossed from Indiana into Ohio, and any of five that crossed from Ohio into Pennsylvania or western Virginia.[26]

In the dozen years between Lincoln's two trips between Springfield and Washington the nation's railroads had improved in the comfort and convenience of travel. By 1860 a passenger could purchase a through coupon ticket from eastern cities to the "far west." Long-distance baggage checking was available on many roads, and train speeds had increased. One could travel from Saint Louis to Boston in forty-eight hours. In the North many of the best trains included "sleepers." Since there were no dining cars yet available, travelers ate hurried snacks at railroad eating houses. The best chair cars were equipped with corner toilets, water tanks, and newsboys. Night travel was prevalent, but Sunday passenger trains were still a matter of dispute, especially in the South.[27]

No uniformity of track gauge existed in 1860; half a dozen different gauges were in use in the thirty-one states having railroads. The standard gauge was quite common in the North, and the five-foot gauge was popular in the South. The strap-iron rail and U rail, still common in the late 1840s, by 1860 had almost totally been replaced by the rolled wrought iron T rail. Most of the T rails used in the late fifties ranged in length from eighteen to twenty-four feet and in weight from thirty-five to sixty-eight pounds to the yard. Steel rails did not appear until the Civil War and after.[28] While there was a great desire to use American rail, the English-manufactured rail remained competitive in price even after $16 a ton in duty was added. Between 1851 and 1856 the Illinois Central purchased eighty thousand tons of fifty-pound English rail for their 705-mile line.[29]

The lack of bridges over major streams still slowed rail traffic. Both Cincinnati and Louisville planned bridges across the Ohio in the 1850s, but none were built below Pittsburgh. At the mouth of the Ohio a two-hour connection was required between William Osborn's Illinois Central at Cairo and Columbus, Kentucky, the northern terminal of the Mobile and Ohio. The two major bridges built during the fifties were Henry Farnam's Rock Island bridge across the Mississippi, and the suspension bridge near Niagara Falls completed by Augustus Roebling in 1855.[30]

Significant improvements in locomotive design and performance appeared during the 1850s. There were changes in boiler design, cylinders, fuel, and general weight and size. In matters of wheel arrangements, however, there was no change because most railroads still largely depended on the American type (4-4-0) with its bogie truck in front and four connected drivers. Such an engine with brass trim and bright paint, a balloon stack and large headlight, carried a name rather than a number and was the pride and joy of the engine crew assigned to it. But, between 1850 and 1860 the typical American locomotive acquired larger cylinders, increased in weight from fifteen to twenty-five tons, and boasted a higher steam pressure.[31]

Most of the five hundred or so locomotives built each year in the country were manufactured by three eastern builders: Thomas Rogers, Matthias Baldwin, and the three Norris Brothers—Richard, Septimus, and William.[32] Some of the best-looking engines came out of the small shop of William Mason, who once wryly said that locomotives should look somewhat better than cook stoves on wheels. Few of the new locomotives built in the decade cost more than $10,000. In 1856 William Osborn, the president of the Illinois Central, was expecting to pay Morris K. Jesup of New York City only from $9,000 to $9,500 for each of twenty "coal burners with copper furnaces." During the decade, most railroads were still using cord wood for fuel, although a few progressive roads were successfully converting to coal. Most wood in the Old Northwest ranged in price from $2 to $5 a cord during the decade.[33]

Freight and passenger cars together probably outnumbered locomotives by a ratio of more than fifteen to one. In turn, freight cars outnumbered passenger cars by a ratio of at least eight to one. The typical freight car had two four-wheel trucks, was from twenty-six to thirty-four feet long, had a capacity of from eight to ten tons, and rarely cost more than five hundred dollars to build. The typical freight train was rarely more than fifteen cars in length, normally had a payload of little more than one hundred tons, and probably had an average speed of no more than ten miles an hour.[34]

Passenger cars in the fifties were constructed of wood and were normally about fifty feet in length, nine to ten feet in width, with a seating capacity of fifty to sixty. Most cars still depended upon candles for illumination since many company officials frowned on the use of oil lamps because of the danger of fire. Heat came from a wood or coal burning stove at one end of the car. J. Richard Beste, a visitor from England, was happy to find a water closet in his railroad coach since it "removed one great difficulty, which the father of eleven children could not but have foreseen, in this journey of three hundred and twenty-five miles. . . ." First class passenger coaches in the late fifties could cost from $2,000 to $5,000 each.[35]

Of course, the new sleeping cars were even more expensive. By the mid-fifties, several varieties of sleeping cars had been invented by predecessors of George M. Pullman. Some of the new cars were quite luxurious, but none of them seemed to solve fully the problem of nighttime ventilation. In May, 1859, after arriving in Chicago via a sleeper, Horace Greeley wrote: "After gasping a while [*sic*] like a netted fish on a hot sandbank, I . . . enter my solemn protest against all sleeping-cars not provided with abundant . . . ventilation." However, that same spring, Richard Cobden spent two nights in sleeping cars between New York City and Chicago "with little fatigue."[36]

Even though rail passenger and freight service of the 1850s was far from perfect, it offered many advantages over the rival canal boat and river steamer. Water freight rates were lower than those of the railroad, but this advantage was to a degree offset by the fact

that rail routes were often shorter. Even the slow-moving freight
train was faster than a canal boat or most steamboats. Canals were
closed from three to five months each winter, and river traffic was
often stopped by floods or low water. Railroads, on the other hand,
were open fifty-two weeks a year. Finally, rail routes were far more
extensive in mileage on the eve of the Civil War than either canal
or river routes. Most interior towns in Ohio, Indiana, and Illinois
started to grow and prosper only with the coming of the railroad.
None of those three states' capitals—Columbus, Indianapolis, and
Springfield—ever had any significant steamboat service. All three
cities started to grow and prosper with the coming of railroads.

The peak of canal construction had come in the 1830s, and new
construction had definitely slowed in the 1840s. By 1850 American
canals extended 3,700 miles, but during the fifties more mileage
was abandoned than constructed. In 1850 Ohio, with 792 miles of
canal, ranked third in the nation and Indiana, with 214 miles, was
fifth.[37]

In Indiana the Wabash and Erie Canal reached Lafayette in
1843, Terre Haute in 1849, and Evansville in 1853. Even by 1851,
total canal expenditures in Indiana were greater than receipts. In
1852 Lafayette obtained rail service to Indianapolis. Four years later
a railroad running parallel to the upper Wabash River, and the canal,
was completed from Fort Wayne west through Lafayette and on
into central Illinois. Rail passenger service was then available from
Lafayette to Toledo in nine hours, six times faster than the canal
packet. Hoosier canals were quickly bested by the Iron Horse, and
even some captains of steamboats on the Wabash began to hedge
their bets.[38]

Ohio canal traffic also declined. Ohio canal packet business
quickly gave way to rival rail service. Between 1851 and the mid-
1850s, Ohio canal tolls dropped from $833,000 to $500,000 a year.
Between 1852 and 1860, canal commerce arriving at Cleveland
dropped from 425,000 tons to only 122,000 tons, and in the same
years Toledo's canal traffic dropped 50 percent. In March, 1857,
the *American Railroad Journal* noted a serious decline of Ohio canal
traffic because of the railroads.[39]

Western river steamboats also were successfully challenged by
railroads in the fifties. Louis C. Hunter in his *Steamboats on the
Western Rivers* (1949) sees steamboat travel declining in "the Criti-

cal decade" of the fifties partially because of "the increasing diversion of traffic to the railroads. . . ." Railroad distances were shorter and schedules faster than those of the side-wheeler or stern-wheeler. Between Cincinnati and Saint Louis, the Ohio and Mississippi Railroad moved freight 339 miles in thirty hours, while by steamboat the 702-mile trip took three days. In 1857 the *American Railroad Journal* noted that the Ohio and Mississippi Railroad passenger service had "broken up the business of the daily [steamboat] line" between Saint Louis and Louisville. Railroads provided comparable savings in time and distance between Cincinnati and Nashville, Cincinnati and Pittsburgh, and many other cities. As a result, such cities as Cincinnati, Louisville, and Pittsburgh saw little or no growth in their steamboat traffic during the decade while their rail traffic doubled several times.[40]

Railroad service had other advantages over riverboat traffic. Railroads set up and maintained regular schedules, avoiding departure delays so common with river traffic. Railroads also provided greater flexibility for shippers, since, within limits, cars could be added or dropped to fit available traffic.[41]

For three decades prior to the mid-century, western steamboats had a real monopoly on transportation in the Mississippi-Ohio basin. The many east-west rail lines built in Ohio, Indiana, and Illinois during the 1850s broke this riverboat monopoly, especially north of the Ohio. The four great trunk lines (New York Central, Erie, Pennsylvania, and Baltimore and Ohio) and their extensions in western states were built to serve eastern rather than southern markets. This major rail construction in the Old Northwest soon resulted in a new east-west trade axis which replaced the earlier north-south trade of the Ohio and Mississippi steamboats.

During the 1850s the railroads of the nation helped the entire national economy achieve a new orientation and posture. Agriculture underwent several significant changes because of the expanding rail network. In the twenty years between 1840 and 1860 there was a marked shift in the center of grain production from the East to the Old Northwest. In 1860 Illinois led the nation in both wheat and corn production, and Chicago forwarded to eastern markets 700,000 barrels of flour, 12,400,000 bushels of wheat, and 13,700,000 bushels of corn.[42]

As the center of farming shifted to the West, so did the growth of population. During the 1850s, the population of the Old North-west and the states just to the west simply exploded, increasing by 68 percent, nearly double the national rate. A review of the early business career of Cyrus McCormick reveals that in Illinois during the fifties there was a close relationship between the sale of reapers, the increased production of wheat, and the building of railroads. Certainly by the eve of the Civil War very few farmers in Illinois, Indiana, and Ohio were more than twenty or twenty-five miles from a railroad. The natural co-operation between prairie railroads and agriculture was noted by the English traveler James Stirling: "... the prairies absolutely make their own railways without cost to anyone . . . the railway improves the land; the improvement pays for the railway."[43]

The expansion of industrial and manufacturing activity in the northeastern states easily matched the agricultural surge of the Old Northwest. The first maturing of American industry accompanied the construction of new rail lines to the west. As the major trunk lines were built westward to the Ohio River and then on to the Mississippi, the exchange of western food for eastern manufactured goods rapidly increased. American manufactured goods of the fifties were rich in variety and were gaining fame for their quality. The railroad spikes made in Pittsburgh, the brass clocks produced in Connecticut, the sturdy picks and shovels manufactured by Oakes and Oliver Ames in Massachusetts, the popular Concord coaches out of New Hampshire, the plows pouring out of John Deere's factory in Moline, Illinois—all were produced in such quantity that they required a mass market. Such a market needed the reliable year-round transportation made available by the newly built railroads.[44]

The thousands of miles of new railroad between the Hudson and the Mississippi River resulted in a new east-west trade axis which was replacing the earlier north-south trade of the Mississippi and Ohio steamboats. As the western trade expanded during the decade, the older merchant capitalism gave way to an emerging national economy centered more on domestic than foreign trade. The men of business and commerce in Boston, New York City, Philadelphia, and Baltimore, no longer so preoccupied with foreign trade, were increasingly shifting their attention from dock and wharf to the railroad depot and freight yard.[45]

The Civil War found the western states allied politically as well as economically with the Northeast. In the elections of 1860 and 1864 the five states of the Old Northwest voted for Lincoln and the Republican party, a party they had earlier helped to create. Even though Copperheads were strong in southern Ohio, Indiana, and Illinois, all three states responded to the call to the colors better than most northern states. But the building of many iron roads throughout the Old Northwest during the 1850s was also a major factor. This point is graphically made by William and Bruce Catton in their *Two Roads to Sumter:*

> Southerners who dreamed that the Northwest might be neutral or even an ally in the event of civil conflict should have looked more closely at the endless parade of freight trains clattering across the mountains between the ocean and the Lakes.[46]

Clearly the most significant railroad construction during the fifties occurred in the Old Northwest, especially in Ohio, Indiana, and Illinois. These iron roads to western states quickly became a new east-west axis of commerce between the industrial and mercantile East and the agricultural West. These new railroads were to achieve an early maturity as they helped their region face the challenges of a great civil conflict.

NOTES

1. *Chronology of American Railroads, Including Mileage by States and Years* (Washington, D.C.: Association of American Railroads, 1953), p. 1.
2. *Ibid.*
3. Edward Chase Kirkland, *Men, Cities, and Transportation: A Study in New England History, 1820–1900* (2 volumes. Cambridge, Mass.: Harvard University Press, 1948), I, 156.
4. Poor's *Manual of Railroads*, 1890, p. vi; *Chronology of American Railroads*, p. 7.
5. Poor's *Manual of Railroads*, 1890, p. vi.
6. Roy P. Basler (ed.), *The Collected Works of Abraham Lincoln* (8 volumes plus index. New Brunswick, N.J.: Rutgers University Press, 1953–1955), II, 31–38; William E. Baringer, Earl S. Miers, and C. Percy Powell (eds.), *Lincoln Day by Day: A Chronology, 1809–1865* (3 volumes. Washington, D.C.: Lincoln Sesquicentennial Commission, 1960), II, 8–10; *American Railroad Journal*, March 10, 1849, p. 159; Louis C. Hunter, *Steamboats on the Western Rivers: An Economic and Technological History* (Cambridge, Mass.: Harvard University Press, 1949), pp. 658–61.

7. Poor's *Manual of Railroads*, 1890, p. vi; *American Railroad Journal*, January 10, 1857, p. 27.

8. Poor's *Manual of Railroads*, 1890, p. vi; United States Bureau of the Census, *Eighth Census* (1860), *Statistics of the United States*, p. 331.

9. *American Railroad Journal*, November 16, 1850, p. 727.

10. United States Bureau of the Census, *Eighth Census* (1860), *Statistics of the United States*, pp. 329–31.

11. Poor's *Manual of Railroads*, 1882, pp. 544–45; Alvin F. Harlow, *The Road of the Century* (New York: Creative Age Press, 1947), pp. 263–74.

12. Poor's *Manual of Railroads*, 1882, pp. 514, 554–55.

13. Gayle Thornbrough et al. (eds.), *The Diary of Calvin Fletcher* (8 volumes to date. Indianapolis: Indiana Historical Society, 1972–   ), III, 409; *American Railroad Journal*, September 25, 1852, p. 613, April 21, 1855, p. 246.

14. Poor's *Manual of Railroads*, 1882, pp. 544–45; *American Railroad Journal*, January 3, 1852, p. 9, March 6, 1852, p. 148.

15. Frederic Logan Paxson, *The Railroads of the 'Old Northwest' before the Civil War* (Wisconsin Academy of Science, Arts and Letters, *Transactions*, XVII, Pt. 1, 1911), pp. 243–67; Poor's *Manual of Railroads*, 1883, pp. 674–76.

16. *American Railroad Journal*, April 14, 1849, p. 233, May 31, 1851, p. 341; Poor's *Manual of Railroads*, 1886, pp. 155–56.

17. Edward Hungerford, *The Story of the Baltimore & Ohio Railroad, 1827–1927* (2 volumes. New York: Putnam, 1928), I, 307–11.

18. Poor's *Manual of Railroads*, 1887, p. 485; Paxson, *The Railroads of the 'Old Northwest,'* pp. 269–71.

19. *Annual Report of the Illinois Central Railroad*, 1856; John F. Stover, *History of the Illinois Central Railroad* (New York: Macmillan, 1975), pp. 37–57.

20. *American Railroad Journal*, March 5, 1859, p. 152, February 11, 1860, p. 127, March 16, 1861, pp. 209–10; Poor's *Manual of Railroads*, 1882, pp. 671–72.

21. Poor's *Manual of Railroads*, 1887, p. 996; *American Railroad Journal*, September 27, 1856, p. 617.

22. Poor's *Manual of Railroads*, 1887, p. 390; *American Railroad Journal*, July 18, 1857, p. 452, October 19, 1861, p. 731.

23. "Internal Improvements" in *De Bow's Review*, XIII (September, 1852), 305; *Weekly National Intelligencer*, March 7, 1857; Allan Nevins, *Ordeal of the Union* (2 volumes. New York: Charles Scribner's Sons, 1947), II, 192.

24. Paxson, *The Railroads of the 'Old Northwest,'* pp. 269–73; *American Railroad Journal*, February 4, 1854, p. 76, June 28, 1856, p. 406; Poor's *Manual of Railroads*, 1882, p. 713.

25. Victor Searcher, *Lincoln's Journey to Greatness* (Philadelphia: Winston, 1960), map on inside cover.

26. George Rogers Taylor and Irene Neu, *The American Railroad Network, 1861–1890* (Cambridge, Mass.: Harvard University Press, 1956), maps at end of the book.

27. Lillian Foster, *Way-Side Glimpses, North and South* (New York:

Rudd & Carleton, 1860), pp. 119–20; Thomas Low Nichols, *Forty Years of American Life* (2 volumes. London: J. Maxwell and Co., 1864), II, 9; Alfred Bunn, *Old England and New England* (London: R. Bentley, 1853), p. 146.

28. Carl R. Fish, "The Northern Railroads, April 1861," in *American Historical Review*, XXII (1917), 786; Robert C. Black III, *The Railroads of the Confederacy* (Chapel Hill: University of North Carolina Press, 1952), p. 13; Thomas Weber, *The Northern Railroads in the Civil War, 1861–1865* (New York: King's Crown Press, 1952), p. 6.

29. *American Railroad Journal*, September 1, 1849, p. 550, August 5, 1854, pp. 481–82.

30. *Ibid.*, February 4, 1854, p. 71, November 5, 1853, p. 717, March 4, 1855, pp. 187–88, June 30, 1855, p. 403, September 3, 1859, p. 566; Foster, *Way-Side Glimpses*, pp. 66–68.

31. *American Railroad Journal*, July 9, 1853, p. 437; John H. White, Jr., *American Locomotives: An Engineering History, 1830–1880* (Baltimore: Johns Hopkins Press, 1968), p. 486.

32. White, *American Locomotives*, pp. 20–21, 449–50, 453, 456–57.

33. *American Railroad Journal*, June 10, 1854, p. 360; W. H. Osborn to J. Newton Perkins, October 30, 1856, Illinois Central Archives, Newberry Library, Chicago.

34. *American Railroad Journal*, May 15, 1852, p. 308, July 12, 1856, p. 437, February 26, 1859, p. 138, November 12, 1859, p. 59, October 20, 1860, p. 922; J. L. Ringwalt, *Development of Transportation Systems in the United States* (Philadelphia: Published by the author, 1888), p. 308.

35. Ringwalt, *Development of Transportation*, p. 162; August Mencken, *The Railroad Passenger Car* (Baltimore: Johns Hopkins Press, 1957), pp. 22–25, 42–54; J. Richard Beste, *The Wabash or Adventures of an English Gentleman's Family in the Interior of America* (2 volumes. London: Hurst and Blackett, 1855), I, 110.

36. Mencken, *The Railroad Passenger Car*, pp. 59–64; Horace Greeley, *An Overland Journey from New York to San Francisco in the Summer of 1859* (New York: C. M. Saxton, Barker & Co., 1860), pp. 7–8; Elizabeth H. Cawley (ed.), *The American Diaries of Richard Cobden* (Princeton, N.J.: Princeton University Press, 1952), p. 163.

37. George Rogers Taylor, *The Transportation Revolution, 1815–1860* (New York: Rinehart & Co., 1951), pp. 52–53, 79.

38. *American Railroad Journal*, December 13, 1851, p. 797, January 29, 1859, p. 83.

39. Harry N. Scheiber, *Ohio Canal Era: A Case Study of Government and the Economy, 1820–1861* (Athens: Ohio University Press, 1969), pp. 387, 390; *American Railroad Journal*, January 10, 1852, p. 22, March 7, 1857, p. 147.

40. Hunter, *Steamboats on the Western Rivers*, pp. 481, 490–91; *American Railroad Journal*, June 27, 1857, p. 412.

41. Hunter, *Steamboats on the Western Rivers*, pp. 500–501.

42. Fred A. Shannon, *America's Economic Growth* (New York: Macmillan Co., 1940), pp. 256–57; S. P. Chase, "Foreign and Domestic Commerce

of the United States," *Senate Executive Documents,* 38 Cong., 1 Sess., No. 55, p. 148.

43. Nevins, *Ordeal of the Union,* II, 169; James Stirling, *Letters from the Slave States* (London, 1847), p. 11.

44. Nevins, *Ordeal of the Union,* II, 172–74, 248–50; Nichols, *Forty Years of American Life,* I, 380–81.

45. *American Railroad Journal,* September 22, 1860, p. 839, December 22, 1860, p. 1124, August 31, 1861, p. 618.

46. William Catton and Bruce Catton, *Two Roads to Sumter* (New York: McGraw Hill, 1963), p. 67.